In celebration of our 100th Anniversary, Nashua Trust Company is proud to dedicate this book to the citizens of our community—past, present and future.

To the new, we hope this publication will serve as an historic guide through the rich heritage of our city.

To longtime residents, we offer this book as a keepsake and reminder of a city that prospered and grew because of your commitment and dedication.

We also wish to extend our thanks to Florence Shepard and Brian Lawrence. Their untiring efforts and fine work have resulted in a book that will be treasured by many in years to come.

•

Nashua Trust
An Amoskeag Bank

NASHUA
NEW HAMPSHIRE

a·pictorial·history

by Florence Crosby Shepard
photographic editor: Brian Lawrence

THE
DONNING COMPANY
PUBLISHERS
NORFOLK / VIRGINIA BEACH

To the memory of Frank Ingalls
and all the photographers and artists
who through their images
have left a very special record
of the history of our city.

Copyright © 1989 by Florence Crosby Shepard
and Brian Lawrence

All rights reserved, including the right to reproduce this work
in any form whatsoever without permission in writing from the
publisher, except for brief passages in connection with a review.
For information, write:

       The Donning Company/Publishers
       5659 Virginia Beach Boulevard
       Norfolk, Virginia 23502

Edited by Veronica Kirk
Richard A. Horwege, Senior Editor
Book design by Sherri Faye Caldow

Library of Congress Cataloging-in-Publication Data:

Shepard, Florence Crosby, 1914-
  Nashua, New Hampshire: a pictorial history/
by Florence Crosby Shepard; photographic editor
Brian Lawrence.
    p.   cm.
    Bibliography: p.
    Includes index.
    ISBN 0-89865-769-5 (lim ed.)
    1. Nashua (N.H.)—History—Pictorial works. 2. Nashua
(N.H.)—Description—Views. I. Lawrence, Brian, 1960-   .
II. Title.
F44.N2S52   1989   89-1606
974.2′8—dc 19   CIP

Printed in the United States of America

CONTENTS

FOREWORD

To quote Henry James, "the power to guess the unseen from the seen, to trace the implication of things, to judge the whole piece by the pattern, the condition of feeling life in general so completely that you are well on your way to knowing any particular corner of it—this cluster of gifts..." is what Florence Shepard brings to *Nashua, New Hampshire: A Pictorial History*. In this book she introduces the people, places, events, and institutions that make up this particular and special corner of the universe.

Using over three hundred illustrations—photographs, drawings, maps, portraits, and postcards—she records not only the past decade but also uncovers artifacts discovered in an archeological dig, pointing to the existence of a seasonal camp in Litchfield as far back as thirty-five hundred years!

In this pictorial history the reader meets "some representative nineteenth century Nashuans" such as Anne Mason Morrill and Albin Beard, and makes the acquaintance of people as grand as Daniel Abbot, the "father of Nashua," and as humble as the city employee who cleaned up after several hundred horses in the street. He encounters the earliest grave in the Old South Burying Ground, that of Elizabeth Weld in 1687, and the site of the "oldest apple tree in New England." He is a witness to such significant events as the Centennial Parade, the Crown Hill fire of 1930, and the closing of the mills in 1948.

The author points out that as early as 1851 Nashuans craved cultural enrichment and thus formed the Union Atheneum, a lending library and sponsor of lecture series involving such eloquent orators as Oliver Wendell Holmes and Stephen Douglas. That legacy is evident in organizations like the Nashua Symphony Orchestra, now in its sixty-fifth season.

John H. Gage was a Nashua inventor, machinist, and industrialist. He operated the tool factory for the cotton mills, the first in the country where machinists' tools were made. Gage was also a shrewd businessman who by 1851 had formed his own company, Gage, Warner and Whitney. Born in 1815, he died in a hunting accident in 1862. He was prominent in community affairs, served in the legislature, and was a colonel in the militia. This portrait, The Gage Family, *was painted in 1846 by the well-known artist, Joseph Goodhue Chandler (*Antiques Magazine, *November 1972, page 849; color reproduction of the painting, September 1983, page 487). It shows Gage, his wife Catherine, and their two sons, Julius who fought in the Civil War and Edward who died young.*
Courtesy of the National Gallery of Art, Washington; gift of Edgar William and Bernice Chrysler Garbisch

In her discussion of architects Asher Benjamin (who laid out many of the streets) and Ralph Adams Cram (whose Gothic Revival Hunt Library is on the National Register of Historic Places), she demonstrates reverence for fine architecture. With her we mourn the demise of the Willow Spring saltbox on Daniel Webster Highway South, of the city's only crescent building, the Montcalm, of the Yankee Flyer diner, and of the Beasom House on Main Street. At the same time we celebrate the restoration of the Merchants Exchange and anticipate the construction of Gateway Center.

On the subject of the Merchants Exchange project, Ms. Shepard states that it "defines the city's character as a place that respects the past even while building the future." It is perhaps this grasp of the critical connection between the past and future that enables her to record so vividly the evolution of the city from the tiny town of Dunstable to the burgeoning metropolis of nearly eighty thousand people.

Nashua, New Hampshire: A Pictorial History is a work that defines the city's character in a manner that is simply unmatched.

Caroline Mason,
Special Assistant to Mayor James W. Donchess

ACKNOWLEDGMENTS

The author and photo editor wish to thank all those who have given assistance and encouragement while this book was being compiled. They are especially grateful to the Nashua Public Library for the use of materials in its collection.

Among the persons who lent photographs, most of which had never been published before, were the following: Paul Newman, Margaret Beasom Swart, Frank Mooney, Nancy Atherton Buell, Janet Atherton Snow, Blanche Nutting Bickford, Patty Ledoux, Eleanor Balcom, Richard and Jean Carson, Meri Reid, Jeannine Levesque, Richard and Ruth West, Mrs. James Walsh, Don Hamel, Renée Dube, Robert Pinsonneault, Alice McWeeney, and John Lafazanis. We also appreciated the interest that was shown by several individuals who offered pictures we were not able to use. The assistance by Mr. and Mrs. Frank Mellen in procuring information on archeology was most helpful.

The author would like to express her appreciation to Alfred and Lorraine Lawrence of Cameraland for their courtesy and patience that helped to solve problems and keep up morale. Al generously opened his back files, proving that a photographic store that has been in business for many years is an excellent source for a book such as this.

The author thanks her family, co-workers, and friends for their understanding during a period when her time was largely absorbed by this project.

The Old South Burying Ground, along with the Old Brick Schoolhouse, appears here in the serene setting that existed long before Royal Ridge Mall was built. The earliest grave in the burying ground is that of Elizabeth Weld, the minister's wife, who died in 1687 at the age of thirty-one. Many other very early inhabitants of the town are buried here, including all of the men who were killed in an encounter with Indians on September 5, 1724. The inscription on the stone marking their grave reads: "This man with seven more that lies in this grave was slew all in a day by the Indiens." Four of the men from Dunstable were Thomas Lund, Ebenezer French, Oliver Farwell, and Ebenezer Cummings. The other four were from outside the town.
Courtesy of Alfred Lawrence

PREHISTORY TO • A.D. • 1775

In the 1840s a young Nashua lawyer, Charles Fox, wrote *The History of the Old Township of Dunstable*, a classic among New England town histories (Gill, 1846, Heritage reprint, 1983). Fox took a brief look at the geology of the area and made this comment: "At some remote period the greater portion of these valleys must have been covered with water in the form of lakes or large ponds." Today it is known that glaciers advanced and retreated over this entire region from about one million to fourteen thousand years ago. As temperatures warmed, the meltwater filled depressions in the terrain. Modern geologists have given the name "Ancient Lake Merrimack" to the largest of these glacial lakes. They call another that extended over present day Nashua and Hollis "Ancient Lake Nashua."

An essay on the geology of Nashua was included in the *History of the City of Nashua* by Parker (Telegraph Publishing Co., 1897). The author, Henry B. Atherton, used as a symbol of glacial action the huge boulder in the Pennichuck woods known as Simonds Rock.

The warming trend that melted the Laurentian ice sheet continued for some time, resulting in much milder weather than at present. Gradually average temperatures declined and brought about the present climate.

Human habitation was not possible until the age of ice had permanently disappeared. Archeological studies in the Merrimack Valley have been undertaken only in recent years; much more needs to be done to round out the knowledge of the aboriginal cultures that lived here. In 1930 Warren K. Moorehead conducted a survey which uncovered evidence of Indian burials along the banks of the Merrimack River on the Hudson side. Unfortunately, Moorehead apparently ran out of funds before he could investigate Nashua sites (*The Merrimack Valley Survey*, Peabody Museum, 1931).

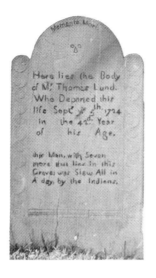

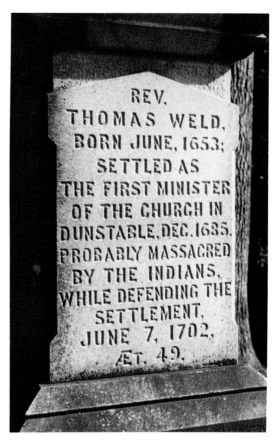

Thomas Lund was the son of the first Thomas Lund who came to Dunstable about 1680. Here is the stone that marked his grave and also served as a memorial to the eight men killed in the famous Indian incident. It occurred far up in the North End when they went in pursuit of Indians who had abducted two of their fellow townsmen while they were collecting pitch from pine trees. The massacre was a great shock to the town which by that time, 1724, felt relatively free from fear of attacks. Lund, aged forty-two, left a family of five children. NPL file photograph

Separate gravestones were erected for two of the men who were killed on that fateful day in 1724: Oliver Farwell and Ebenezer Cummings. Both were young men, Farwell was thirty-three and Cummings was twenty-nine, and both left young children. Photograph by Brian Lawrence

In 1875 a monument to Thomas Weld and Nathaniel Prentice was erected in the Old South Burying Ground. They were the first two ministers of Dunstable. For some inexplicable reason the lines "probably massacred by the Indians while defending the settlement" were added to Weld's inscription. There was no war being waged in 1702 so this is simply not true. Photograph by Brian Lawrence

Important information was gained in the late 1960s from excavations carried out prior to construction of a new Amoskeag Bridge in Manchester. The exciting result was proof through radiocarbon dating that man had lived in the Merrimack Valley for at least eight thousand and possibly as long as ten thousand years (Dincauze, *The Neville Site,* Peabody Museum, 1976).

In 1982 a dig was undertaken when preparations for a new fish hatchery in nearby Litchfield uncovered cultural remains. It was discovered that this spot on the eastern bank of the Merrimack had been a seasonal camp as far back as thirty-five hundred years ago. In late spring and early summer native groups had regularly visited the area to gather and process plant materials that were important to their subsistence (Kenyon, *The Smolt Site,* Peabody Museum, 1983).

The 1988 issue of the *New Hampshire Archeologist* contains important new information on other sites in Litchfield that have been investigated. The seasonal nature of native habitation in the area was confirmed in these later discoveries in 1983 and 1984 (Bunker, *Two Woodland Components in Litchfield, New Hampshire*).

In late 1987 state archeologists discovered an undisturbed cultural site near the Hilton Inn in Merrimack. With the help of volunteers they have found many artifacts, including flakes and actual tools, from a camp that may have existed for a short period of time about seven thousand years ago (*The Telegraph,* July 26, 1988).

The late Charles Lund, whose ancestral home was on Robinson Road, left a collection of about 150 Indian artifacts that were found on his land and that of his neighbors. These are now owned by the Nashua Historical Society. Archeologists found that the collection reveals important clues, stating in their report: "Evidently the locale was continuously occupied from the Middle Archaic through the late Woodland periods." This covers an expanse of time from about 6000 B.C. to A.D. 1600 (Kenyon, *The Lund Collection: Nashua, New Hampshire*, N.H. Archeology Society, 1985).

The archeologist Chester Price published a map in 1968 that showed the routes of all the Indian trails. He indicated that the Indians definitely had a small camping ground in the present Nashua area that they called Watanic (a variation of this name is Watanonock). The

Here is the flat stone, completely covering the grave, that was laid down in 1687 over the burial spot of Elizabeth Weld. Since this was the very first grave dug in the burying ground, the flat stone may have been a precaution against wild animals disturbing it. It is not in a position that is easy to photograph, however. Elizabeth was a descendant of distinguished ministers and came up from Boston to Dunstable in 1681 when she married. She bore four children in five years. Two of her children had died the year before—they may be buried here also but there is no indication of this on the stone.
Photograph by Brian Lawrence

The stone erected in memory of Benjamin Cutler was professionally carved by a Lowell stonecarver. Cutler was the original owner of the farm that the town bought in 1828 for use as a town farm.
Photograph by Brian Lawrence

Indians were probably members of the Souhegan or Naticook tribe. When the explorers, Willard and Johnson, canoed up the Merrimack seeking the river's source in 1652, they observed natives along the shore between the mouths of the Nashua River and Salmon Brook. This occurred in the month of August when the fishing was probably at its best.

A state law now requires archeological surveys for the sites of public works construction before the bulldozers destroy cultural evidence. In 1984 an archeological study of Nashua was finally published. It was funded by a matching grant from the National Park Service and was administered through the New Hampshire State Historic Preservation Office. It includes a report on investigations of the Pheasant Lane Mall site which concluded that at one time there may have been a quartz workshop there. Other sites were the Thoreau's Landing area at the confluence of the Merrimack and Nashua rivers, the vicinity of the Iron Works on Salmon Brook, Mine Falls, and the routes of several interceptors.

The people called Indians crossed a land bridge from Asia to Alaska in prehistoric times. They spread south-

ward and eastward until some of them reached the Atlantic coast. The story of how they populated the United States and Canada would make a saga of heroic proportions if it had been written down as it developed. Among some groups it was passed down orally from one generation to another. In 1854, for example, a member of the Mahican tribe gave this account:

A great people came from the Northwest, crossed over the salt waters and, after long and weary pilgrimages (planting many colonies in their track) took possession and built their fires upon the Atlantic coast, extending from the Delaware on the south to the Penobscot on the north. They became in process of time divided into different tribes and interests, all, however, speaking one common dialect. This great confederacy held its Council once a year to deliberate on the general welfare.

(Whipple, *The Indian and the White Man in New England,* 1976).

This statement may suggest how the great Algonquian nation developed. The North American Indians

The mid-nineteenth-century gravestones of
Clifton and Rebecca Lund have embossed
lettering which suggests that no expense
was spared by their children in memorial-
izing "Our Mother" and "Our Father."
Lund was a descendant of the first Thomas
Lund in Dunstable and also of the one
killed in 1724. He is listed in a city directory as a "yeoman," a rather old-fashioned
term to designate a farmer. His farm was
on the Lowell Road.
Photograph by Brian Lawrence

The most touching headstone in the burying ground is this one for a baby son of
Nathaniel and Mary Prentice. The carved
heart surrounding the inscription adds a
poignant touch, expressing the sorrow of
the parents who laid him away here so long
ago. From the date on the tombstone it is
known that less than three weeks later the
minister would be called upon to give
comfort to the families of the men killed in
the massacre.
Photograph by Brian Lawrence

were divided into six linguistic groups, of which the
Algonquian was one. All of the Indians in New England
were part of the Algonquian family. The particular tribe
that lived in southern New Hampshire, northern Massachusetts, and part of eastern Vermont was the Pennacook.
East of them was the territory of the Sokokis and north of
the Sokokis were the Abnaki, "the people of the dawn."

In 1837 the town changed its name from Dunstable to
the name of its river, Nashua. The Indian group that
originally named the river was not based in this locality;
their main village was where the river rises. Nashaway,
in fact, was an early name for Lancaster, Massachusetts.
To these Nashaway Indians it meant in their language
"beautiful stream with a pebbly bottom."

Three great Pennacook leaders were Passaconaway,
his son Wonalancet, and his grandson Kancamagus. All
wanted peaceful relations with the English. Before he died
Passaconaway transformed his own physical decline into
a symbol of the decline of his race in these words:

The oak will soon break before the whirlwind. I

commune with the Great Spirit. He whispers to me
'Tell your people Peace, Peace is the only hope of your
race... The palefaces shall live upon your hunting
grounds and make their villages upon your fishing
places.' We must bend before the storm! The wind
blows hard! The old oak trembles!

The Pennacook presence haunts the background,
forming a continuity to the prehistoric past when aborig-
ines of unknown roots made their homes here. The
Indians, for example, named Salmon Brook because it was
the source of a fish they especially enjoyed. These original
settlers of our land are still shadowy figures but we now
have a somewhat clearer picture of their lifestyle from the
hearths, implements, tools, and fragments of pottery that
have survived centuries of burial.

The first English to become familiar with this area
were fur traders. Several trading posts were set up to buy
fur, much in demand in England, from the Indian trap-
pers. One of these fur traders, Joseph Wheeler, became a

Lt. Timothy Bancroft was born in 1709 and died, as the inscription says, on November 21, 1772. He came to Dunstable in 1730 and owned the large farm that was right on the state line although most of his property was in Massachusetts. His military title was by virtue of service in Col. Eleazer Tyng's company in 1754. His son, Ebenezer Bancroft, was a hero at Bunker Hill.
Photograph by Brian Lawrence

Col. Joseph French was a descendant of Samuel French who came to Dunstable in 1680. He was a colonel in the militia.
Photograph by Brian Lawrence

member of the community that was set up; in the absence of any records about other very early inhabitants within the limits of present day Nashua, he is usually designated Nashua's first resident.

During the 1660s Judge Edward Tyng foresaw that this was the next frontier and bought land in what is now Tyngsborough. Looking even further ahead, Tyng also foresaw that some day the Merrimack Valley would be a major industrial region. His son, Jonathan Tyng, built a house and managed the Tyng estate for many years; he was a leading citizen of "Ancient Dunstable."

An example of a grant made by Massachusetts in Nashua was the thousand acres ceded to the Ancient and Honorable Artillery Company in 1673. By the early 1670s enough people owned land, obtained mostly through grants, to formally organize the territory into a township. Nashua has three birthdays: its charter making it a part of this large township, its charter making it by itself a New Hampshire town, and its charter as a city. The first of these was October 26, 1673, when a two hundred-square-mile rectangle of land was declared a Massachusetts township, subsequently named Dunstable be-

cause of connections that the Tyng family had with the English town of that name. The first town meeting was held at Wheeler's house in May 1674.

It should be emphasized that this did not come about because a group of people already settled in the area petitioned the Massachusetts General Court to declare them a town. Out of the twenty-six men who signed the petition for a charter, Tyng and perhaps two or three others were actually living in the area. The rest were Boston, Salem, and Concord merchants who had been given grants, plus Chelmsford people who were glad to have another town established on their northern border. This group constituted the "Proprietors" who would encourage worthy families to come as pioneers to civilize and conquer the wilderness.

There is one clue that suggests that a few of the land-owners had recruited individuals to make homes in the area somewhat earlier. That clue was maturing apple trees discovered by those who came after 1673. It is quite possible that short-lived attempts at settlement had been made, the persons concerned abandoning the effort because of the isolation, fear of Indians, and the harshness

According to the 1800 census records there were two Benjamin Smiths living in Dunstable. They were father and son, so the one whose gravestone is shown here was actually Benjamin Smith, Jr. His father was listed by Fox as taking part in the Revolution; he was also a delegate to the convention to write a constitution for New Hampshire. The younger Benjamin was an ensign in the army; "ensign" was an army rank at that period. He was probably a member of the militia. The neatly inscribed lines at the bottom of the stone speak eloquently about Smith's character:

A husband kind, a parent dear,
A neighbor just, a friend sincere,
Confessed by all with him acquainted,
He liv'd belov'd and died lamented.

Photo by Brian Lawrence

The beautiful decoration on Deacon Thomas Colburn's stone is still fresh after two hundred years. He was ninety-six years old when he died, an unusual longevity at that period.
Photograph by Brian Lawrence

of the winters. There are no documents to prove this, however, and the "apple tree mystery" will probably never be solved.

During the first fifty years of the city's history the tiny frontier settlement faced repeated setbacks because of wars that posed the threat of Indian attacks. In 1680 Dunstable had a population of thirty families. In 1701 during a peaceful interlude a petition asking for financial assistance from the provincial government stated that the number of families was twenty-five. In 1711 during the dangerous garrison period at the time of Queen Anne's War, there were only thirteen families.

The great event that occurred in 1725 was Lovewell's War which stopped the threat of Indian attacks. The great hero was the legendary John Lovewell who was killed as he led a small group of stalwart fighters in a battle with the Pigwacket Indians at what is now Fryeburg, Maine.

The second fifty years saw many changes. Starting around 1730 the ancient township broke up into separate communities as the farther reaches of the area became settled and the frontier moved on. Most of these towns are now included in what is called the Greater Nashua area—Hollis, Hudson, Merrimack, Milford, Amherst, and Brookline among them.

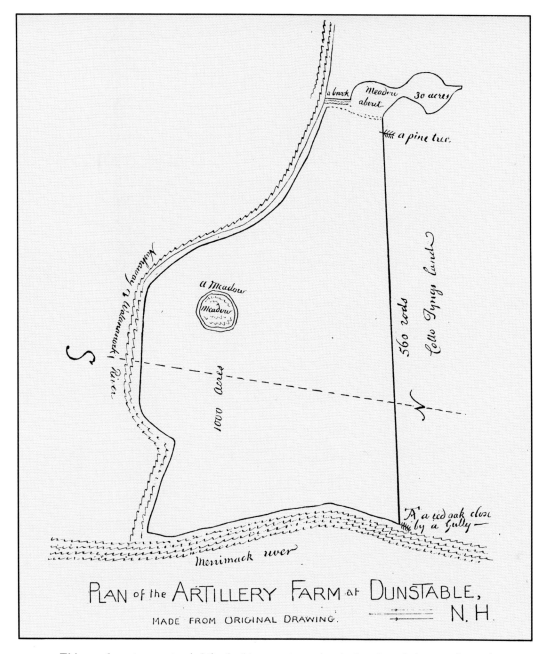

a brook

Meadow about 30 acres

a pine tree

Nashua or Watannuck River

a Meadow

Meadow

560 rods

Collo Tyngs land

S

N

1000 acres

"A" a red oak close by a gully—

Merrimack river

PLAN of the ARTILLERY FARM at DUNSTABLE, N.H.

MADE FROM ORIGINAL DRAWING.

This rough map accompanied the deed to the "Artillery Farm" when it was granted by the province of Massachusetts to the Ancient and Honorable Artillery Company. In 1673 the area was a great pine forest with a marshy section on the southern side. The "red oak close by a gully" and the pine tree at either end of the northern boundary have, of course, fallen long ago. This boundary probably ran through what is now Greeley Park. The Artillery Company did very little to develop its property—in fact the only interest they took in it was to request that a tenant farmer pay them rent in the form of apples for their supply of cider. The thousand acres of land was eventually sold to Colonel Joseph Blanchard whose heirs fought a law suit over the mortgage.

Roberts, History of the Military Company of Massachusetts now called the Ancient and Honorable Artillery Company of Massachusetts, 1637-1888, *published in 1895*

When the state line was run in 1741 and Massachusetts no longer had any claim to this region, there was a period of confusion, an identity crisis—which colony did the town belong to, Massachusetts or New Hampshire? Governor Benning Wentworth answered this question in 1746 by chartering Dunstable, New Hampshire. The town at that time had a population of about four hundred. Except for a boundary dispute with Hollis, in the settlement of which about five hundred acres of land were lost, its total area was the same as it is today.

Religious dissension and education of children were two problems confronting the citizens. It was not until 1774 that money was finally appropriated to build schoolhouses in five districts. Suddenly the town found itself caught up in fast-moving political events in the outside world—the Declaration of Independence and the Revolution.

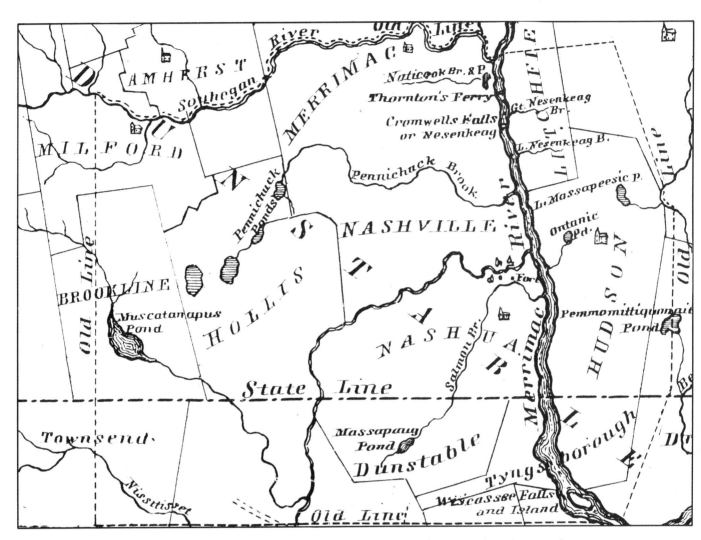

This is the map that appeared in the first history of Dunstable/Nashua, written by Charles J. Fox. On a contemporary map of the 1840s he superimposed a delineation of the boundaries of the "Ancient Dunstable" of 1673. The designation "Nashville" referred to the North End that formed its own town government in 1842. The towns included in the rectangle were those in present-day Greater Nashua plus several towns and parts of towns now in Massachusetts. After the state line was drawn in 1741, there were two "Dunstables" and the confusing situation of two towns next door to each other having the same name continued until one changed its name to Nashua in 1837.

An unknown artist drew this imaginary sketch of the First Meetinghouse and some of the homesteads in the settlement of Dunstable. The exact location of the little log church is unknown but it was near the Salmon Brook in the "Harbor" area. This is probably a fairly accurate representation of the original village from which the city of Nashua has grown. Note the fencing around the houses, a feature stipulated in the "Agreement" drawn up to regulate the management of the individual land holdings. These early citizens believed firmly that "good fences make good neighbors." NPL file

The Second Meetinghouse is marked by this inscription on a plaque set into a boulder at the approximate location near the front of the burying ground. The larger and probably somewhat more comfortable church was built when the First Church was officially organized in 1685. The Reverend Thomas Weld, who had been in Dunstable for several years, was the first minister and his parsonage was nearby. As was customary, a burying ground adjacent to the church was soon laid out. The Daughters of the American Revolution placed the plaque on the spot in 1900. Photograph by Brian Lawrence

This is a sketch of the last meetinghouse built by the town of Dunstable, along with a floor plan that shows the arrangement of the pews. The church was located at the triangle on lower Main Street near Rivier College. A marker erected by the DAR

indicates the site where it stood from 1754 until 1812. Soon after this latter date, separation of church and municipal government went into effect. NPL file

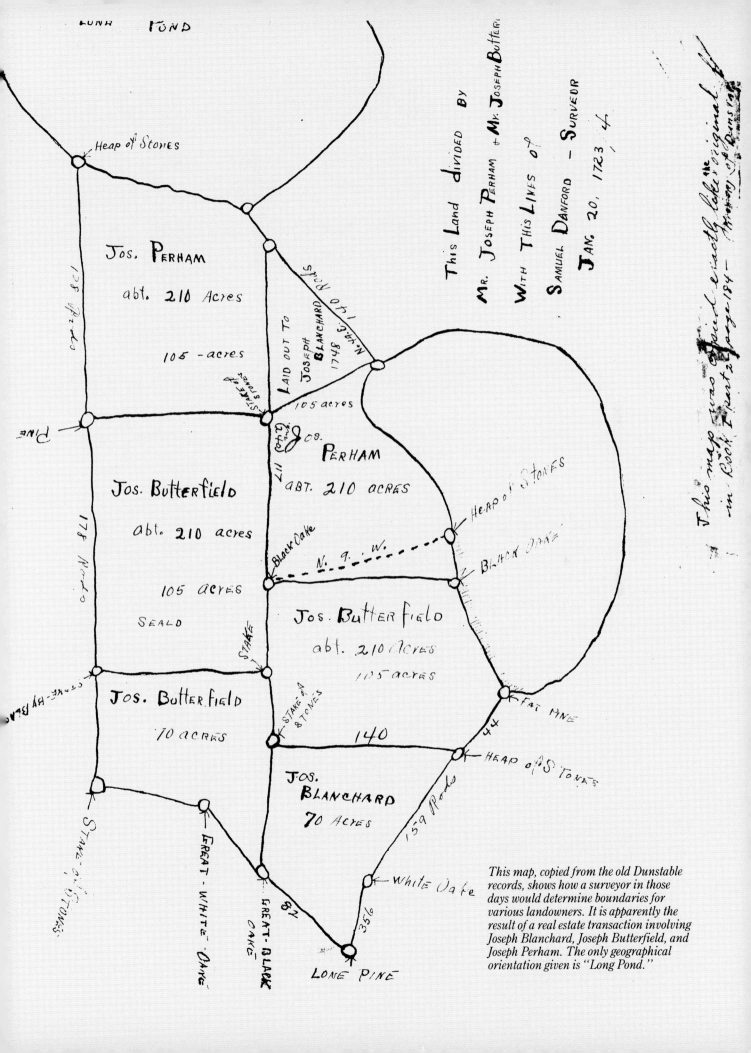

LONG POND

Heap of Stones

JOS. PERHAM
abt. 210 Acres
105 - acres

JOS. BUTTERFIELD
abt. 210 acres
105 ACRES
SEALD

JOS. BUTTERFIELD
70 ACRES

LAID OUT TO JOSEPH BLANCHARD
1748 130 Rods

105 acres

JOS. PERHAM
ABT. 210 ACRES

Black Oake

N. 9. W.

Heap of Stones

BLACK OAKE

JOS. BUTTERFIELD
abt. 210 acres
105 acres

FAT PINE

44

STAKE

STAKE OF STONES

140

HEAP OF STONES

JOS. BLANCHARD
70 ACRES

159 Rods

STAKE OF STONES

GREAT - WHITE - OAKE

GREAT - BLACK OAKE

82

WHITE Oake

356

LONE PINE

This Land divided by Mr. Joseph Perham & Mr. Joseph Butterfi
With This Lines of Samuel Danford - Surveur
Jan. 20, 1723 4

This map is two traced exactly like original
in Cook Tract page 184 — Anthony of Dunsta

This map, copied from the old Dunstable records, shows how a surveyor in those days would determine boundaries for various landowners. It is apparently the result of a real estate transaction involving Joseph Blanchard, Joseph Butterfield, and Joseph Perham. The only geographical orientation given is "Long Pond."

ON THIS POINT OF LAND DWELT
JOHN LOVEWELL,
ONE OF THE EARLIEST SETTLERS
OF DUNSTABLE, AT WHOSE HOUSE
HANNAH DUSTON
SPENT THE NIGHT AFTER HER
ESCAPE FROM THE INDIANS
AT PENACOOK ISLAND
MARCH 30, 1697.
———
ERECTED BY
MATTHEW THORNTON CHAPTER, D.A.R.,
1902.

The monument on Spaulding Street indicating that "Hannah Duston slept here" marks the approximate location of the house of John Lovewell, patriarch of the famed Lovewell family. He operated a sawmill on Salmon Brook. His son was the John Lovewell who faced the Pigwacket Indians on their home grounds in Maine. Hannah's overnight stay may be legendary. NPL file photograph

This map, showing the exact location of the fort built by the Massachusetts authorities in the fall of 1702, appears in a booklet, Historic Nashua: A Few Notes from Local History, *written by Mary Josephine Hodgdon, a Nashua school teacher, in 1902.*

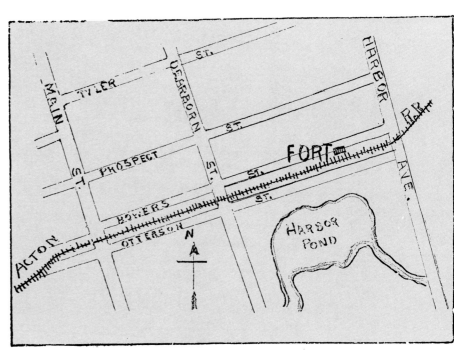

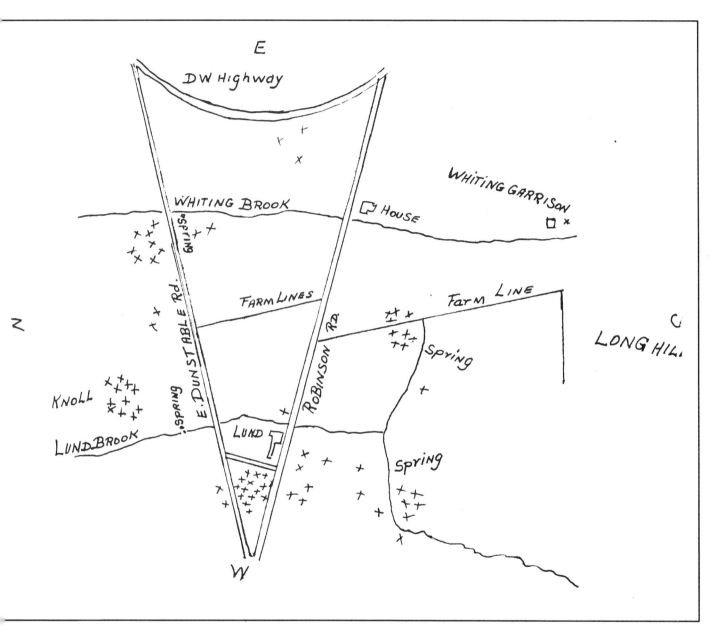

E

DW Highway

WHITING BROOK

WHITING GARRISON

HOUSE

FARM LINES

FARM LINE

Spring

LONG HILL

C

N

KNOLL

Robinson Rd.

E. DUNSTABLE Rd.

spring

spring

LUND BROOK

LUND

Spring

W

Charles Lund—farmer, antiquarian, and descendant of an early settler—drew this map to show the locations of some of the Indian artifacts found on his land and that of his neighbors. In four places he has noted "spring." Does the presence of artifacts near springs mean that Indian groups may have set up temporary camps near these sources of water? If these places were used on repeated visits, discarded parts of weapons such as arrows and spears, stone tools, and broken pottery might have accumulated. Lightly buried, many of them were later turned up by plowing or tree-cutting. All of the objects in the Lund Collection as a whole were discovered during the 1870s and 1880s, according to records at the Nashua Historical Society.

An attempt has been made to correlate the names of landowners as given by Lund with an 1872 map. A general pattern emerges, pointing to Nashua's southeastern corner as a territory frequented by Indian groups who may have traveled up the river from the south in canoes. Information courtesy of Frank Mellen; original map from NPL file

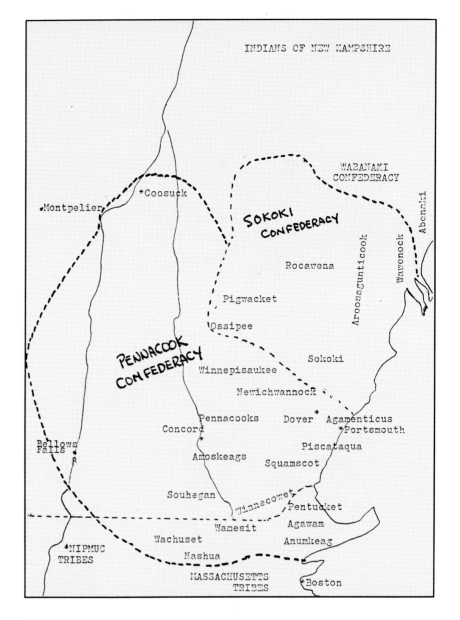

INDIANS OF NEW HAMPSHIRE

WABANAKI CONFEDERACY

SOKOKI CONFEDERACY

PENNACOOK CONFEDERACY

Montpelier
*Coosuck
Rocawena
Pigwacket
Ossipee
Aroosagunticook
Wawenock
Abenaki
Sokoki
Winnepisaukee
Newichwannock
Pennacooks
Dover *Agamenticus
Concord
*Portsmouth
Piscataqua
Bellows Falls
Amoskeags
Squamscot
Souhegan
Winnecowet
Pentucket
Wamesit
Agawam
Wachuset
Anumkeag
*NIPMUC TRIBES
Nashua
MASSACHUSETTS TRIBES
*Boston

This map outlines the territories occupied by three great Indian confederacies before the coming of white settlers. It appeared in a publication called Historical Indian-Colonial Relations of New Hampshire, *published by the Pennacook-Sokoki Inter-tribal Nation in 1977.*

In the fall of 1987 state archeologists discovered evidence of cultural remains on an undisturbed site near the Hilton Inn in Merrimack. With the help of volunteers they spent several months carefully excavating in the area and have come up with some exciting artifacts such as tools made by very early people from various kinds of stone. The conclusion reached is that it was a place occupied for a brief period as far back as seven thousand years ago. Archeology is a painstaking science involving definite steps that are taken to pinpoint the exact location and level where artifacts are discovered. A very small amount of soil is removed at a time and is screened so that any artifacts can be separated. The trained eye of the professional archeologist can tell if what appears to be an ordinary piece of stone was actually shaped by a human hand as part of a tool. The technique of radiocarbon dating is also used to date finds such as charcoal from ancient fires or shards of pottery. Courtesy of the photographer, Dean Shalhoup, and the Telegraph

In 1945 and 1946 the Nashua Telegraph *ran a very informative series of articles by an author identified only as "the Old Timer." This illustration by an unknown artist was used for his account of the origin of the Nashua trademark, the Indian head. He says, speaking of the aftermath of the September 4, 1724 massacre on the north side of the Nashua River: "The Indians, elated with their success, moved forward to the Nashua River and the second fight took place at the ancient fordway near the present Main St. Bridge. . . . Tradition reports that the Indians were on the north side of the river with the settlers holding firm on the south side. . . . The Indians upon their departure had carved a crude outline of an Indian's head upon a large oak as a mark of defiance. Such was the origin of Indian Head."*

"Indian Head" as a symbol caught on very quickly. In the area near the scene of the fight, the "ancient fordway," the name Indian Head Village was used. Much later the Jackson Mills would become famous for their Indian Head cloth; they adopted this symbol as a trademark. When a bank was started in Nashville, it took the name Indian Head. When this same bank erected a new building in 1924 it incorporated the symbol into the sculptured decorations on the exterior. In this photo one can see clearly how the image was used at the top of the columns. In 1929 the bank commissioned Curtis Dallin, great sculptor of Indian figures, including the statue in front of the Boston Museum of Fine Arts, to provide the Indian head over the entrance.
Courtesy of Jeannine Levesque who has made a specialty of aiming her camera upward at architectural details on the buildings of Nashua

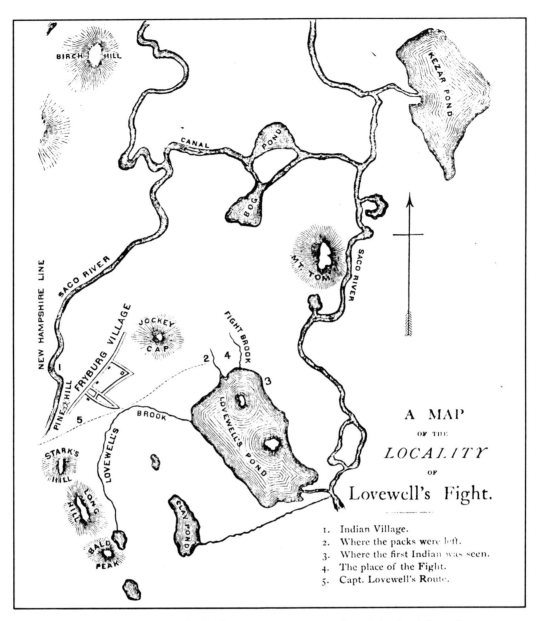

BIRCH HILL

KEZAR POND

CANAL

POND

BOG POND

MT. TOM

SACO RIVER

NEW HAMPSHIRE LINE

SACO RIVER

JOCKEY CAP

FRYEBURG VILLAGE

FIGHT BROOK

PINE HILL

BROOK

LOVEWELL'S POND

STARK'S HILL

LOVEWELL'S BROOK

LONG HILL

CLAY POND

BALD PEAK

A MAP
OF THE
LOCALITY
OF
Lovewell's Fight.

1. Indian Village.
2. Where the packs were left.
3. Where the first Indian was seen.
4. The place of the Fight.
5. Capt. Lovewell's Route.

Just across the New Hampshire/Maine line is the place where Lovewell's fight with the Pigwacket Indians occurred. In May 1725, John Lovewell of Dunstable led fifty men on a march northward to attack the Indians on their home grounds. Out of ten men from Dunstable itself, only two survived a bloody battle beside the pond shown on the map. The town of Fryeburg, Maine, is named after the chaplain who was among those slain. An eighteenth-century ballad written about this event ends with these lines:

> *"Sad was the hour and terrible*
> *When Lovewell brave*
> *   'gainst Paugus went*
> *With fifty men from Dunstable."*

Map from The Expeditions of Captain John Lovewell *by Kidder*

The Willow Spring House may have been built as early as 1685 but there seems to be no actual proof of that. It was located on the east side of the Daniel Webster Highway, just north of the state line, adjoining the Bancroft property. Members of the Bancroft family owned it at various times. A spring of exceptionally pure water at the site gave the house its name. One owner bottled the water in the form of a ginger ale. In later years the house was a gift shop. Its last owner was Dr. Clarence Bent, the well-known veterinarian. Knowing the location of this charming old saltbox structure, it is not hard to guess its fate—it was demolished when preparations were being made for the building of Pheasant Lane Mall. Photograph from Robinson, Old New England Houses

The "1700 House" is now the oldest house in Nashua. Here is how it looked around 1920. Recent owners have lovingly restored it and it is a cherished landmark on the Dunstable Road just south of the Robinson Road junction. It was built by a Mr. Killicut and is also sometimes referred to as the "Blodgett House." This priceless museum piece that has seen almost three hundred years of the area's history pass its door should be preserved even if the traffic of the present-day world has to make a slight detour to go around it. Courtesy of Nancy Atherton Buell

Here is the "1700 House" as it looks today after restoration. Photograph by Brian Lawrence

Little is known about this very old house that stood for many years at the beginning of Lake Street where Bailey's Nurseries and Florist Shop was later located. It may have dated back to the middle of the eighteenth century, according to the only information available.
NPL file photograph

The John Searles House on Searles Road was Dunstable's first school. In the back wing classes were held after 1746 for part of the year, alternating with another house at the North End where school was also kept. This was the best that the rather impoverished citizens could do in the way of providing instruction for their children. There were no actual schoolhouses built until the 1770s. This house was torn down in the 1950s.
NPL file photograph by Frank M. Ingalls, famous Nashua photographer

The house known as "the Haunt" on Davis Court has been in three different locations during its 250 years. It was originally built in Dunstable, Massachusetts, then it was moved to Hollis where it acquired a reputation for being haunted. William Spalding, who owned the Abbot House, bought the house and moved it to Nashua around 1905 as a place to display his antique collection. It is now a privately owned residence.
NPL file photograph

The Nashua area has several restaurants that are also historic houses. On Amherst Street is the Country Tavern. This lovely ancient farmhouse and barn have been tastefully restored by the same people who own Common Crossing downtown. It even has a friendly ghost named Elizabeth! She was the owner of the house in 1874—her full name was Elizabeth Ford. A special feature of the place is that it boasts the oldest apple tree in New England. There is very little information available about former owners that can be documented, but it is definitely known that the main part of the house was built in 1741.
Courtesy of Meri Reid

This photograph is a valuable collector's item. The Lund House on Robinson Road is shown as it looked before the barn burned down. Still another Thomas Lund built the house in 1767-1768, planing and finishing all of the woodwork himself. It is the oldest two-story house in Nashua. The style is typical center-chimney colonial.
Courtesy of Frank Mooney

29

The portrait of Daniel Abbot appears in Parker's History of Nashua. Nothing is known of the portrait painter, whose name, "Guterunst," can be barely made out in the lower lefthand corner. The present whereabouts of the original painting is also unknown. The picture presents a photographic impression of a personality marked by kindliness and sagacity. Abbot, "the Father of Nashua," was born in Andover in 1777 and graduated from Harvard in 1897. He studied law in Salisbury, practiced for a short time in Londonderry, and then came to Nashua where he spent the rest of his busy life. In addition to his work in starting the Nashua Manufacturing Company, Abbot was the first president of the Nashua and Lowell Railroad, a legislator, and was involved in other enterprises in both town and state. He died in late 1853, having lived long enough to see Nashua become a city.

2

1776 · TO · THE INDUSTRIAL REVOLUTION

In 1775 New Hampshire conducted a census to determine the military resources available in the province. Dunstable had a total population of 705, 325 of whom were females of all ages. An interesting statistic was the counting of "seven negroes and slaves for life." (All slaves were automatically freed when the state constitution was ratified in 1784).

The town contributed to the full extent of its manpower and finances toward the winning of the War for Independence. About 163 men fought in the military forces. Sixteen of these were casualties. After the war had been won, Dunstable, its population even less than before the war, settled down to life as a rather obscure farming village. The leading families were still the Lovewells, the Blanchards, and the Lunds. Hollis had almost twice as many people. When the time came to select a county seat for Hillsborough County, Amherst won.

Excerpts from the town records give some idea of the main concerns of the people during this transitional period.

"May 7, 1776: Voted to pay Dea. Thomas Lund four shillings for transporting one Aaron and wife and two children from Dunstable to Bedford." (This referred to the policy of solving the welfare problem by sending impoverished persons out of town. Often they were "warned out"; in this particular case the family may have had relatives in Bedford and transportation was arranged for them.)

"March 3, 1777: Voted that thirty pounds be raised for schools." (This was a 50 percent increase over what had previously been spent on the five schools set up in town.)

In 1802 Daniel Abbot bought this house that today, especially when spotlighted at night, gives so much charm and romantic elegance to the area at the top of Library Hill. It has been widely admired as an outstanding example of the Federalist style of architecture. In 1978 the Nashua Historical Society bought the house when Miss

Sylvia Spalding, the last surviving member of the family that had owned it, died. With the help of many citizens, the society renovated the interior, restoring it to the period when the Abbot family was living there. It is the only house-museum open to the public in Nashua.
NPL file photograph

"April 10, 1777: Voted that the town treasurer be and is hereby directed to hire as much money at six percent per annum as will be wanted to pay the extraordinary expenses of raising the proportion of men in the town for the Continental Army."

"February 9, 1778: Voted to appoint a committee of nine to give Jonathan Lovewell instructions to call a full and free representation of this state for the sole purpose of framing and laying a permanent plan or system for the future government of this state."

"September 9, 1779: Met for the purpose of taking under consideration the Bill of Rights and plan of government for the State of New Hampshire."

"September 20, 1779: Voted to reject the Bill of Rights."

"October 10, 1781: Voted that fifty-five silver dollars be raised to procure rum for the Continental Army."

"January 15, 1782: A vote was proposed to see if the town objected against the plans of government lately formed for the state and it unanimously passed in the affirmative."

"December 23, 1782: Voted that the objections against the Bill of Rights and plans of government as drawn by the committee be as it now stands and that

the selectmen draw off the objections and send the same to Concord." (These votes critical of early drafts of a state constitution were indicative of the vigilant attitude of the people who wanted to have a voice in the new government.)

"March 1, 1784: Voted to allow Thomas Killicut three shillings for the use of the canue at Nashua River Bridge. Voted to allow those men that workt at giting the timber out of Nashua River in March, 1783, £0-3-6 per day. Voted to pay for the rum that was drank when the timber was took out of Nashua River." (The first bridge across the river had been built about 1746 and required much repair work, especially in the spring when freshets damaged it.)

"August 28, 1797: Voted to accept of the road laid out by the Selectmen from the road leading from Dunstable meeting house to Nathan Fisk to the road laid from said meeting house to Thomas Pearson's." (This was the Searles Road.)

"January 15, 1810: Voted to accept the road laid out from Mr. John Whittles towards Hambletts Ferry." (This was East Hollis Street.)

"November 4, 1816: A road was laid out beginning at the Great Road at the south side of Gen. Lovewell's barnyard and running westerly to the Hollis Road."

The Indian Head Coffee House stood on the corner of Lowell and Concord streets for almost ninety years. Built by a man named Timothy Taylor, it was a stage coach stop for many years. When Nashua Manufacturing Company bought up land, it was included in its holdings. Company records refer to it as the "upper tavern" because of its position at the top of a hill. Before it was torn down in 1892 it had

become a Catholic school for girls called St. Rose's Academy. The First Church occupies the exact site. The hotel's ad in the 1845 directory pointed out that "The Indian Head Coffee House on Nashville Square and the elevated observatory upon its top gives the stranger in the place an easy opportunity of seeing the whole village and its vicinity at one view."
NPL file photograph

(This was Lake Street.)

"March 14, 1820: Voted that paupers who reside or who hereafter reside in town...be put up at auction in one lot." (The person who bid the lowest on this transaction did have to follow certain rules for the care of the paupers. This was another way of solving the welfare problem.)

Until 1895 Dunstable was not even served by a stagecoach line. Until 1803 mail was collected at Tyngsborough. After the turn of the century the part of the North End known as Indian Head Village began to develop as a rather lively center. A man named Timothy Taylor built an inn at the corner of Main and Lowell streets. A one-story structure, it was later enlarged to become the Indian Head Coffee House. A lawyer named Daniel Abbot came to town around 1802 and opened an office, bought the house at Abbott and Nashville streets, and established himself very quickly as a civic leader. After the Middlesex Canal was opened, a canal boat was launched on the Merrimack River; on July 4, 1803, Abbot delivered a speech celebrating this event and made his own suggestion concerning the "birthday" of the town. He felt that the center that was

developing just north of the Main Street Bridge should be called Nashua Village. He probably would have liked to have changed the name of the entire town to Nashua as of the date when he was speaking.

The picture which emerges from the historical accounts reveals a town that was divided geographically. There was a substantial village at the "Harbor" or Salmon Brook area where the original settlement had been—this extended down the present Daniel Webster Highway to the state line. Then there was a rather barren stretch of vacant land referred to as the "Dunstable Plains" that was not good for farming because of its very sandy soil. Across the river was the bustling center of Nashua Village. It may be difficult to visualize the present-day busy downtown area as a sandy plain covered with pine trees, but that was what it was like until after the Industrial Revolution had hit the town.

In the early 1820s Abbot and other forward-looking men such as the Greeley brothers had formed a coalition with Boston industrialists and financiers to build mills here. In 1823 the Nashua Manufacturing Company was chartered by the state of New Hampshire. The company bought all the land it thought it might need for this enter-

Charles Lund drew this sketch of the old Allds House from the description of it written by Daniel Webster's sister-in-law, who lived in the house when a child. Built sometime in the eighteenth century, it was torn down in 1816. The location was on Allds Street near Harbor Avenue. Mrs. Webster said: "There was a small entry with doors into the two rooms and stairs in front of the chimney which was in the middle of the house.... The dresser which in other houses was built against the wall of the kitchen was in the house in a corner of the room with a way behind into a dark cellar through a trap door."
NPL file; description in Old Houses, *WPA Historical Project manuscript*

ALLDS HOUSE 17—TO 1816

Here is how one of the earliest schoolhouses built by the town of Dunstable was set up in the interior. The wood for the stove was piled at one end of the entry. Outhouses, one for boys and one for girls, were set up separately at the rear. Plan drawn by Charles Lund, presumably from a description by someone who had attended the school, the District 2 schoolhouse.
NPL file

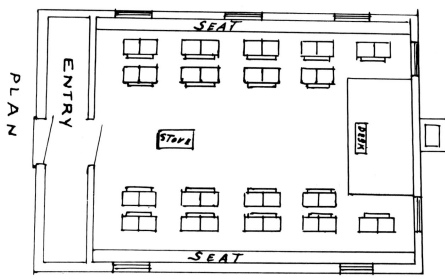

prise and started to excavate a canal from Mine Falls, the source of the water power, to the chosen site for the mills—the south bank of the river just west of Main Street. The original capital was set at one million dollars. One person interested in this endeavor was Abbot's former fellow student in a Salisbury law office, Daniel Webster. Webster subscribed for sixty shares of stock but never paid for it. On record are letters from the treasurer of the company, dunning Webster for the amount he owed.

Suddenly, that strip of sandy land between Salmon Brook and the Nashua River acquired great value. In a very few years well-to-do people had built substantial homes there and hotels and business buildings were going up. Before the end of the century, this land would actually become too valuable for residential use, especially in the area from Hollis Street to the bridge.

The fifty years between the American Revolution and the Industrial Revolution was a time of transition as Dunstable/Nashua moved from its status as a quiet country town to a community that realized it could be something more than that. A fortunate geographical position made this possible—a situation which has continued to the present day.

A memorial plaque on a boulder placed on a knoll at Greeley Park (east side of Concord Street) gives recognition to the fact that there was once a burying ground at this spot. Although the graves and even many of the names of those formerly buried there have disappeared, the stone pays tribute to these very early settlers of the North End. Ira F. Harris spearheaded the movement to put this memorial in place on September 23, 1916.
NPL file photograph

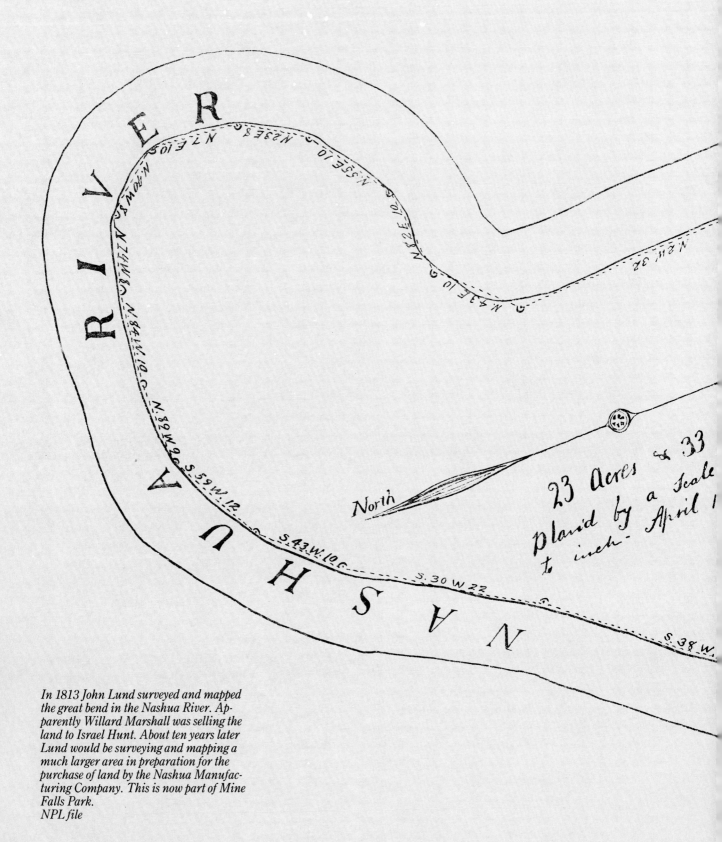

RIVER

NASHUA

N 7 E 10
N 80 W 8
N 23 E 5
N 55 E 10
S 82 E 10
N 43 E 10

N 2 W 32

N 74 W 8
N 88 W 10
N 84 W 10

N 82 W 26

S 59 W 12

S 43 W 10 6

S 30 W 22

S 38 W

North

23 Acres & 33
plan'd by a scale
to inch. April 1

*In 1813 John Lund surveyed and mapped
the great bend in the Nashua River. Apparently Willard Marshall was selling the
land to Israel Hunt. About ten years later
Lund would be surveying and mapping a
much larger area in preparation for the
purchase of land by the Nashua Manufacturing Company. This is now part of Mine
Falls Park.*
NPL file

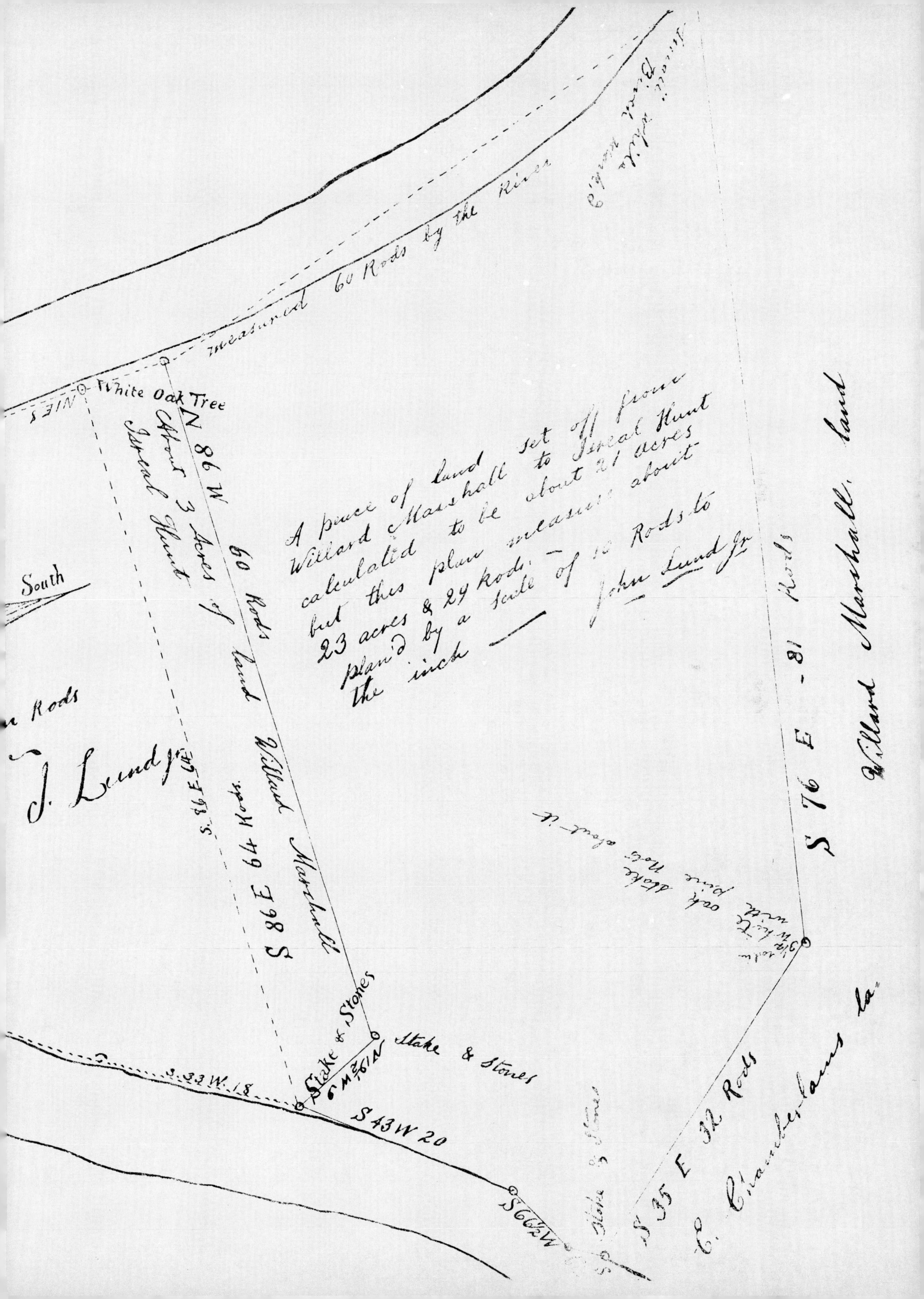

measured 60 Rods by the River

White Oak Tree

N 86 W

About 3 Acres of
Israel Hunt

South

60 Rods Land Willard Marshall

T. Lund Jr

A piece of land set off from
Willard Marshall to Israel Hunt
calculated to be about 21 acres
but this plan measures about
23 acres & 29 rods. -
plan'd by a scale of 10 Rods to
the inch ——— John Lund Jr

S 76 E - 81 Rods

Willard Marshall land

Rods

S 98 E 79 Rods

Stake & Stones

Stake & Stones

N 76 E

S 33 W 18

S 43 W 20

S 66 W

Stake & Stones

S 35 E 32 Rods

C. Chamberlains Land

In 1803 the first post office in Dunstable, New Hampshire, was established at a tavern on the lower "Boston Road." Later it was moved to the Israel Hunt House near the Lovewell House. In 1820 John M. Hunt became postmaster and the third location was his home and store, shown in the photo. Eventually, of course, the post office was moved to the downtown area where it was located at several different places. NPL file photograph

A sketch of the mills of the Nashua Manufacturing Company appeared in Fox's History of the Old Township of Dunstable. Mill No. 1, at the right, was started in 1824 and by early 1825 was finished up to the first floor. The foundations were very deep and solid. By the mid-1840s Mill No. 4 had been built. This is, therefore, how the millyard looked at the time Fox was writing his history.

Fox also included a sketch of the Jackson Company's mills on Canal Street. A close working relationship existed between the two companies, especially in the matter of sharing water rights.

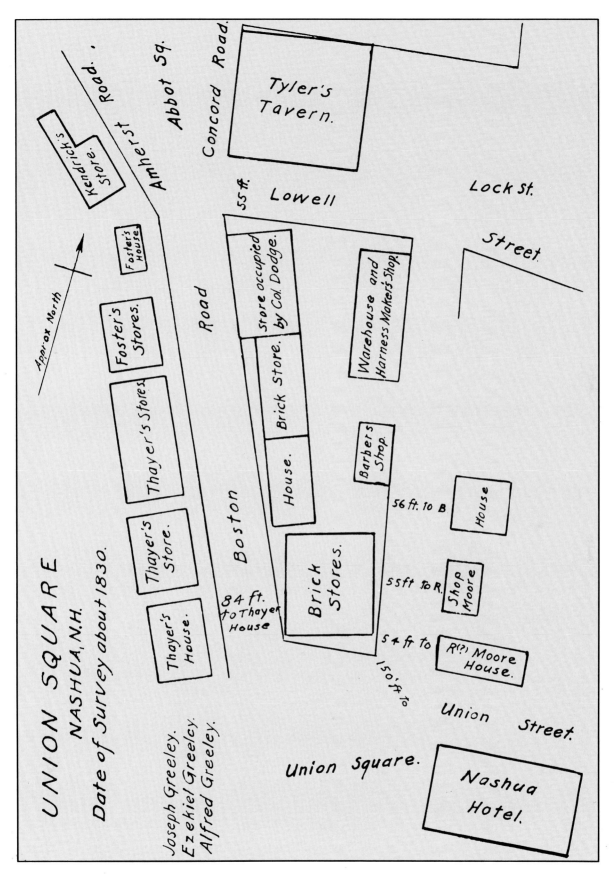

UNION SQUARE
NASHUA, N.H.
Date of Survey about 1830.

Joseph Greeley.
Ezekiel Greeley.
Alfred Greeley.

Approx North

Kendrick's Store.

Foster's House

Foster's Stores.

Thayer's Stores.

Thayer's Store.

Thayer's House.

Amherst St

Abbot Sq.

Concord Road.

Tyler's Tavern.

Lock St.

Street

Lowell

55 ft.

Store occupied by Col. Dodge.

Brick Store.

House.

Road

Boston

84 ft. to Thayer House

Brick Stores.

Warehouse and Harness Makers Shop.

Barber's Shop.

56 ft. to B

55 ft. to R.

5 ft. to

150 ft. to

House

Shop Moore

R(?) Moore House.

Union Street.

Union Square.

Nashua Hotel.

This valuable map provides a picture of the general layout of the area that was known at the time as Union Square. Note that the main street was called the Boston Road. It also shows the exact location of the Nashua Hotel, later the Central House. The three Greeley brothers listed on the lefthand side built and owned the block designated as "brick stores." The map appears to be the result of a surveying job.
NPL file

This is one of the oldest known photographs in the Nashua historical picture collection. The date is possibly early 1850s. All copies were made up to fit oval frames—the photographer was sure that persons buying it would want to frame and hang it. The tall striped pole with the rooster on top is a barbershop symbol. There was, however, a competing barbershop right across the street. By looking closely, one can make out the mortar and pestle and a pair of eyeglasses, advertising a pharmacy, on top of the building at right center. The church was the "Old Chocolate."
NPL file photograph

3

THE · TOWN BECOMES · A CITY: 1825 TO 1900

The stagecoach run between Dunstable and Boston normally took about six hours, but bad weather could slow this time down. The lumbering four-horse-power coaches clattered over the wooden bridge and toiled up the hill now known as "Library Hill." At the Indian Head Coffee House passengers were discharged and horses changed before going on to Amherst and Concord. This stagecoach line was the main communication link with the world beyond the village.

On a winter day in 1825 a passenger on the coach was Asher Benjamin, the new agent for the mills. Early in January Daniel Abbot had recommended to the stock-holders that "an agent should be employed to take a general superintendance of the company's concerns" (Records of Nashua Manufacturing Company, Baker Library, Harvard Business School). His memo went on to praise that mechanical genius, Ira Gay, who was also act-ing as agent, but Abbot pointed out that there was too much work for one man.

It is not known how it came about that a famous architect was willing to come to provincial Dunstable to take this kind of job. Asher Benjamin, although not a great original creator like Bulfinch, had had a brilliant career promoting sound architectural principles and was highly respected as an authority on good design. It has been speculated that he was financially stressed at this point in his life and simply needed a job. He was one of several examples of Abbot's uncanny ability to attract talented men to help him in his great enterprise.

One of the first tasks that Benjamin undertook was the addition of a third story to the "Nashua Hotel" the company had built as a lodging place for single workers. On March 5, 1825, a letter was written by him directing a

This hotel was part of the history of the early days of the Nashua Manufacturing Company and of Railroad Square. Originally built in 1824 as the Nashua Hotel, a third story was added in 1825 when more rooms were needed to house single men working in the mills. Surrounded by elm and Balm of Gilead trees (Nashua Telegraph, August 10, 1895), it stood on what is now Deschenes Oval, facing Main Street. In 1831 NMC sold it and it was renamed the Central House. When in 1845 the land was bought by the town of Nashville as a site for a town hall, the hotel was moved to the north side of the square and an ell was added. The barber whose sign hangs over his shop at the west end was a black man, named Philip O. Ames, described as "of high character and gentle manners, who won and retained the respect and esteem of all." About 1872 a new owner changed the name of the hotel to the Merrimac House. Destroyed by fire in 1876, it was rebuilt as the Laton House.
Photograph made from a spliced negative.
NPL file

carpenter to do this work which would provide ten additional rooms. During the three or four years that Benjamin was here he played an important part in finishing Mill No. 1, starting Mill No. 2, erecting the Olive Street Meetinghouse, and superintending the laying out of streets. The Unitarian Church was started while he was here and the classic design of its building undoubtedly reflects Benjamin's influence.

Daniel Abbot's dynamic personality was a key factor in the beginning of the Nashua Manufacturing Company. His enthusiasm and energy shine through even the dryest report. Not even persistent problems with shoring up the sides of the canal, that "ditch" they had laboriously dug for three miles down from Mine Falls, could dim his optimism, his obvious joy in creating an industry. The town itself was just awakening to its potential and he was leading it, like a Moses, to the promised land of prosperity. It is for good reason that Daniel Abbot has been called "the Father of Nashua."

A few excerpts from the early records will show how rapidly the Industrial Revolution was overtaking a simple farming community:

Jan. 4, 1825—There have been lands purchased since the formation of the company to the amount of $15,800. The rest of the money paid by the company has been expended in the building of the main dam at the head of the Mine Island, the Guard Locks and Gates, the earth dam at the head of the canal basin, laying the foundation of the factory and raising the walls above the first floor, building the machine shop, a store and fourteen blocks of houses...

June 7, 1826—One half of the machinery is in the first factory and the agents expect hereafter to produce from it 2000 yards of cloth per day. The other half of the machinery will probably go into operation next fall, and the second factory will be up and covered before winter.

June 1, 1827—The first factory has 4480 spindles and the second will have 5520, making in both factories 10,000. In the first factory there are 124 looms.

(Records of the Nashua Manufacturing Company, Baker Library, Harvard Business School, Boston.)

Asher Benjamin (1773-1845) was a well-known architect whose books of designs are still used as source material on the architecture of his period. New England churches often reflect his influence. He was a colorful character in the history of the Nashua Manufacturing Company, working here from 1825 to 1827. Daniel Abbot apparently had made his acquaintance through his Boston connections, considered him trustworthy, and offered him a job as agent. It was an interlude in the life of Benjamin that is rather mysterious. He left his stamp on Nashua, especially through the work of his protégé, Samuel Shepherd.
Portrait from
Dictionary of American Portraits

The Olive Street Church stood proudly at the top of Temple Street for about fifty-five years. Daniel Abbot took a personal interest in the building of this church, specifying that it should provide one hundred pews to accommodate townspeople as well as mill workers. He budgeted the cost at $5,000. The photo was taken just before the church was removed from the site in 1881 after being sold for $421. Asher Benjamin undoubtedly contributed his architectural skill to the design.
NPL file photograph

The Unitarian Church was also built during the period when Asher Benjamin was working as the agent of the Nashua Manufacturing Company. It was completed in 1827 and is therefore the oldest church building in Nashua. The building was moved about twenty feet when the parish house was erected in 1929. After the armory next door burned in 1957, the now combined Unitarian and Universalist congregation bought the site and put up the Sunday school and office wing. The cemetery, known as the Nashua Cemetery, was started in 1835; many famous Nashuans are buried there, including Daniel Abbot and Maj. Gen. John Foster.
NPL file photograph

This south-looking view gives another rare glimpse of the Nashua that still had dirt streets. Probably taken in the late 1860s, (Methodist church steeple at far left), it reveals that traffic patterns were so casual that a man could leave his buggy and stop for a chat with a friend in the middle of Main Street.
NPL file photograph

The Boston Clothing Store on the first floor of the first Beasom Block as shown here had an ad in the 1850 directory. This is a very early photo, probably mid-fifties when the flag pole was a prominent feature on Main Street. Beyond the Beasom Block was the Long Block.
NPL file photograph

Three views of the Tremont House show how this famous Nashua hotel looked at different periods. In this view it is seen as it appeared in the 1850s when it was known as the Pearl Street House (Maps of Hillsboro County, New Hampshire, 1858, 1982, reproduction courtesy of Old Maps, West Chesterfield, New Hampshire). The picture is an "ambrotype," an early form of photography, and was produced by a Nashua man named S. B. Richardson whose studio was in the Noyes Block.

The second photo shows the hotel as it appeared after 1868 when the name had been changed to Tremont House. Courtesy of Alfred Lawrence

There was never any question that the name of this firm would be anything but "Nashua," for the river was the source of the power that would turn the wheels and propel the spinning jennies and looms. The river and its energy would turn the town into an industrial center. A system of canals combined with navigation on the Merrimack River would bring the raw cotton grown on southern plantations from the wharves of Boston and convey the finished product, shirtings and sheetings, on the way to markets.

While the new company was selling stock and putting up its first mills, two events marked a transition to a somewhat more urban way of life. The first was the appearance of a newspaper, eventually called the *Nashua Gazette*, late in 1826; it would continue to be published until 1895. In 1832 the present *Telegraph* was started as the *New Hampshire Telegraph*. The two papers struck sparks off each other, enlivening the journalistic scene with opposing political viewpoints. During the middle of the century a third newspaper, called the *Oasis*, published

for a few years. The second important event of the late 1820s was the building of a covered bridge by a private syndicate; it spanned the Merrimack River across to Hudson, replacing the ferries that had provided the only means of crossing for one hundred years.

The 1830s saw intensified industrial activity. The Jackson Company, another cotton mill, was started on the north bank of the river, using buildings previously set up for a woolen mill that went bankrupt. By 1835 Nashua Manufacturing had put Mill No. 3 into operation. Meanwhile hundreds of young girls from the farms had come to work in these mills—this was the era of the "Yankee Mill Girls." The great revolution of this decade was in transportation, as the railroad changed the way people and freight would travel. Nashua's position on a railroad line further enhanced its economic importance.

In 1837 the name of the town was legally changed to Nashua. The 1840s was the period of the "great separation" when, for eleven years, the North End was a town in its own right called "Nashville." The cause of this schism

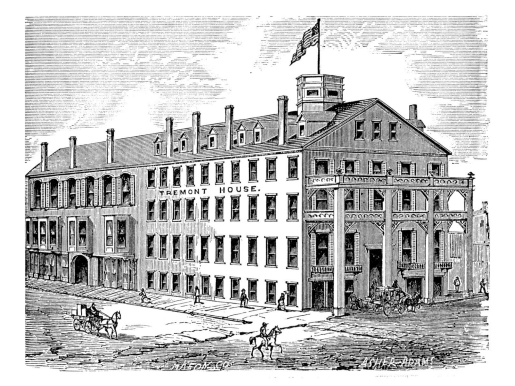

TREMONT HOUSE.

The third view shows how the hotel looked after porches had been added to the front (Early Illustrations and Views of American Architecture by E. V. Gillon, Jr.). Plans for this hotel were announced in the Nashua Gazette *of March 27, 1847: "THE NEW TAVERN—the stock for the erection of a public house on the corner of Main and Pearl Street, $12,000, is all taken up and the enterprise is going ahead,*

sure." The 1850 directory featured an ad for the new establishment so it probably had opened that year or the year before. Then, in the Weekly Telegraph *of October 3, 1874, the announcement is made that Gilman Scripture, an innkeeper who had been mayor of Nashua in 1866-67, had bought the Tremont House and planned to add "a new and beautiful balcony in place of the present portico."*

was disagreement over the location of a proposed town hall. The town had outgrown the informal system of keeping records and conducting municipal affairs from the home of one of the selectmen. The suggestion was made that the old meetinghouse could be moved to a more central place and renovated for this purpose. This frugal idea was rejected as ambitions arose to build an architecturally imposing structure. The presence of a protégé of Asher Benjamin, Samuel Shepherd, meant that local talent was available for the designing and building of a town hall they could take pride in. The citizens of the South End outvoted those of the North End in plans to erect it on the east side of Main Street.

The North End at the time had a population of about three-thousand. Many professional men and managerial employees in the mills had built homes there. Some of them would like to have seen the center of gravity in town affairs shifted to their neighborhood. The Northenders decided to break off relations with the older part of town. With the help of Franklin Pierce (later president of the United States), they became chartered as a completely separate town in 1842.

In 1853 both towns voted for reunion; it was at this time that the city of Nashua was chartered. The first mayor elected was the bobbin maker, Josephus Baldwin, whose home was right across the street from what was now called City Hall.

In 1850 the institution that would become the Penni-

chuck Water Works was started; pipe lines and sewers were extended as home owners and businesses were offered running water. As can be imagined, this gave a boost to the plumbers! In 1858 the town pump, a fixture in Railroad Square for many years, was removed, arousing cries of nostalgic protest from many people. Also during the fifties the Nashua Gas and Light Company was started; by 1860 the gaslight era had come to Nashua and lamplighters lit the street lights every night and extinguished them at dawn.

A sign of a hunger for the cultural side of life was the formation in 1851 of a Union Atheneum. Members paid an annual fee for cooperative buying of books that they could borrow. The Atheneum also sponsored a series of outside lecturers each winter. Some of the big names that came to give talks were Bayard Taylor, Wendell Phillips, Oliver Wendell Holmes, and Stephen Douglas.

In the first half of the sixties the city, like cities and towns everywhere, was involved in the Civil War. There was a certain amount of "Copperhead" sentiment but public opinion quickly squelched these dissident voices. Nashua took great pride in the fact that it over-subscribed its recruiting quota and nine hundred young men marched off to the battlefields, many of them never to return.

In 1867 a further stage in cultural life came about when the Nashua Public Library was established as a tax-supported, free institution. The opening day collection was donated by the Atheneum and the Nashua Manufacturing Company. Space for the library was made available

47

Around 1850 Isaac Spalding, the wealth-iest man in Nashua, built a solid brick house on Main Street. As running water was just starting to be available, he took advantage of the chance to have his house piped for this amenity, the first resident to

do so. The house had a belvidere at the top; covered with ivy, fronted by a lawn and wrought iron fence, it was an imposing residence. It can still be seen behind the Spalding Block of stores. It is now owned by Main Street Methodist Church which uses

it for its Sunday school. The two ladies posing in front perhaps were Isaac's wife, Lucy, and their niece, Sarah Kendall, who lived with them, but their identities are not known for sure.
NPL file photograph

on the second floor of the new County Records Building that had been erected next to City Hall when Nashua became the county seat for Hillsborough County.

The decade of the sixties ended with the inauguration of a daily newspaper, the *Telegraph* having decided that a weekly was no longer adequate to serve the information needs of a fast-growing community. In 1871 the newspaper put up its own building on the corner of Main and Temple streets.

In 1868 a new church spire soared on Main Street as Main Street Methodist Church took its place in the middle of downtown that it has occupied ever since. In 1870 a group of citizens decided that it was time a historical society was formed to preserve the city's heritage. It took a special amendment to their original charter, however, to admit women to membership. Historical Hall was set up in the Telegraph Block as a place for exhibits and meetings.

Suffrage for women was a major topic of controversy during the post-Civil War years. The City Hall auditorium resounded with some sharp debates, many reflecting the disappointment felt by women at being denied even the right to vote in school board elections which the state legislature had supposedly given them in 1869. In spite of repeated protests, Nashua women did not get this privilege until the next century.

The North End continued to be developed as a choice

residential area, with more and more streets being laid out. Family farms were often subdivided and house lots sold. The old pine forests gradually receded, to be replaced by the shade trees that make this part of town such an attractive place in which to live. A number of large farms were in operation even into the present century on the outskirts off both Amherst and Concord streets. A recreational attraction was Mt. Pleasant Riding Park in the vicinity of Artillery Pond. Eventually this would become the North Common.

In the South End many industries flourished during the second half of the century. Although cotton dominated the economic scene, there were also iron and steel works, shoe factories, and numerous small manufacturing concerns that produced everything from hoopskirts to fans. The Nashua Corporation, long known as the Nashua Card board and Glazed Paper Company, started in a very small way in 1848 and grew rapidly during the century.

In 1873 St. Louis de Gonzague Church was built on West Hollis Street by the French community that was becoming an increasingly large segment of the population. After the Civil War, French-Canadians by the thousands immigrated to New England from the farms of Quebec. Nashua was one of the mill towns that attracted them because it offered steady work. A hallmark of this ethnic group was a lifestyle based on the idea of "La Survivance,"

Isaac Spalding's next door neighbor was William D. Beasom. In 1847 Beasom built an outstandingly beautiful residence at 176 Main Street where the Chase Building now stands. Beasom was a merchant and industrialist who came to Nashua in 1831. His family lived in the house until 1913 when his son, William H. Beasom, realized that residential properties in the middle of the downtown area were rapidly increasing in value and placed the house on the market. It was torn down in 1916. The interior finishing of the house was described as matching the magnificence of the exterior.
Courtesy of Margaret Beasom Swart, whose childhood was spent in this house.

This is what the west side of the upper end of Main Street looked like in the 1850s. The residence, with front yard enclosed by a fence, belonged to the first mayor, Josephus Baldwin. To go to his office in City Hall, he just had to cross the street! The original builder of the house was Aaron Fisher who put up the Fisher Building at right. This is another illustration showing how the "bottleneck" came about.
NPL file photograph

meaning that they tried to maintain their traditional language, customs, and religion in the new environment.

A fast-growing population meant, as it does today, that the city government was often faced with the need for new school buildings. In the early seventies the site selected for a larger high school was an old burial ground on Spring Street. The decision was made to exhume the burials and move them to Woodlawn Cemetery. The school that was built there burned down in 1917 and was replaced by the brick building used in recent years as a junior high school. This building was razed recently to make way for the new courthouse.

Among the business structures erected during this period, the Merchants Exchange, completed in 1872, has proved the most durable. Its builder was a coal merchant named Jeremiah White. Many of his associates considered it a risky venture. In 1985 when bricks started to fall from its aging facade, many people feared that this magnificent example of Victorian architecture would have to come down. Fortunately for the historic preservation of downtown, the owners made the decision to give the dowager a facelift. This block now sets a distinctive tone, helping to define the city's character as a place that respects the past even while it is building the future.

Near the end of the decade the Church of the Good Shepherd consecrated its long awaited new edifice which still stands as another gracious feature of lower Main Street.

The census of 1880 counted 13,387 residents in the city. The decade that followed must have been a stimulating time as people found themselves living on the edge of several new technologies such as the telephone and electricity. In newspaper accounts of the period one notes the busy social life and happenings on the business scene that contributed to a general atmosphere of excitement.

Over the years fires have destroyed many fine business blocks. By 1899 the Beasom Block at Factory and Main streets had suffered no less than seven major and minor conflagrations. In 1883 a building was totally destroyed that, in two different locations, had had a very interesting life history. Originally it was a hotel called the Washington House; it stood on the site of the present NFS Savings Bank, between Factory and High Street. In 1853 it was moved to make way for the Noyes Block. At its new location, Bowers and Main streets, it was home to several different industries, including the Nashua Watch Company. Recent excavations for the new medical building for Memorial Hospital uncovered shards of pottery from the

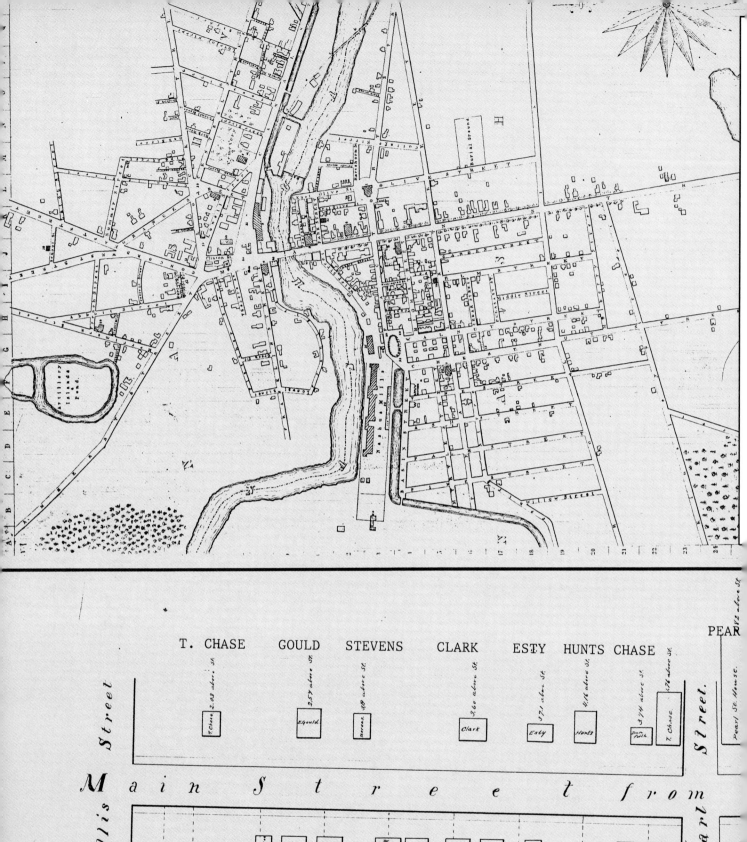

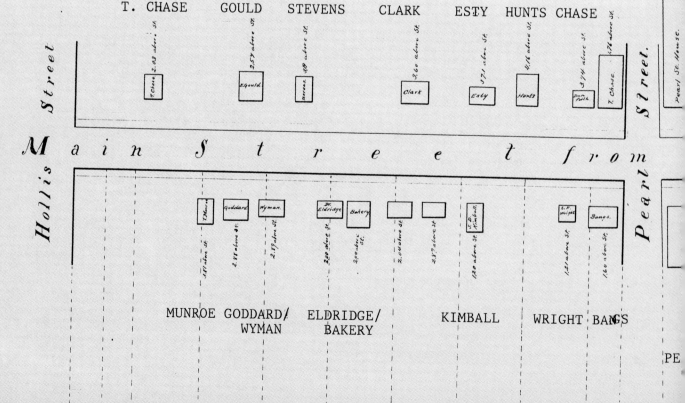

Hollis Street

T. CHASE   GOULD   STEVENS   CLARK   ESTY   HUNTS CHASE

PEAR

M a i n   S t r e e t   f r o m

Pearl St. House.

Pearl Street.

MUNROE GODDARD/   ELDRIDGE/   KIMBALL   WRIGHT BANGS
        WYMAN   BAKERY

PE

MAP OF NASHUA AND NASHVILLE VILLAGES

Surveyed by

J. HOAR & J. MEAD.

1842.

This 1842 map of Nashua/Nashville was the result of surveying done when the two towns separated. In the lower lefthand corner Artillery Pond is depicted as reduced to islands (probably marshy) surrounded by narrow ribbons of water. On the corner of East Pearl and Main streets, the odd-shaped building was the American House, an early hotel that was quite well-known in its day. At that time Factory Street continued across Main Street—the name Temple Street does not appear until 1848. The present Spring Street was called Olive Street. A feature of special interest on this map is that it shows where the canal on the north side flowed into the Nashua River. In this way canal boats could make deliveries right underneath the brick building on the east side of the Main Street bridge. This low entrance is still visible on the back of the building.
NPL file

PLAN
of
MAIN STREET

Surveyed in 1848

by Mead & Butterfield Engineers.

In 1848 another survey was done by a civil engineering firm, apparently to determine elevations on Main Street from Hollis Street to the bridge. Changes have taken place in just six years. The American House has disappeared and on the land it occupied the Pearl Street Church and the Beasom House have been built. Isaac Spalding's house appears on the map although at the time only the foundations may have been in. The Pearl Street House was probably also under construction. Dr. Colburn's office is shown next to his house; later this would become the site of the County Records Building.
NPL file

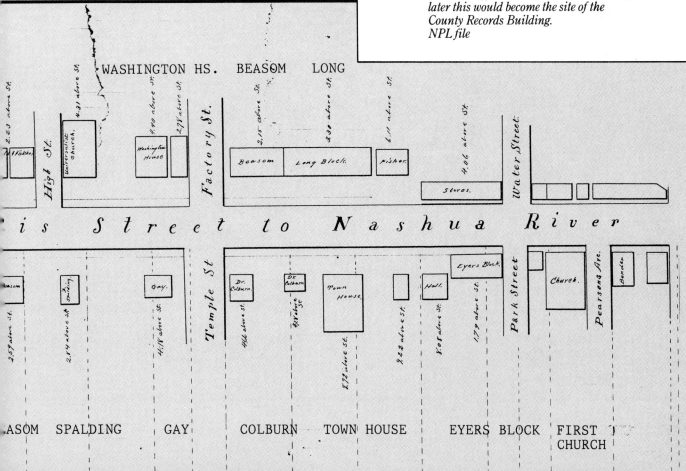

WASHINGTON HS. BEASOM LONG

*By 1858, the date of this map, Nashua's downtown area had become quite thickly settled and more streets were being laid out in the North End. The street designated as West Concord Street is now Manchester Street. Front Street as a residential circle, with a view of the river, is shown clearly (*Maps of Hillsborough County, New Hampshire, 1858, *1982, reproduction courtesy of Old Maps, West Chesterfield, New Hampshire).*

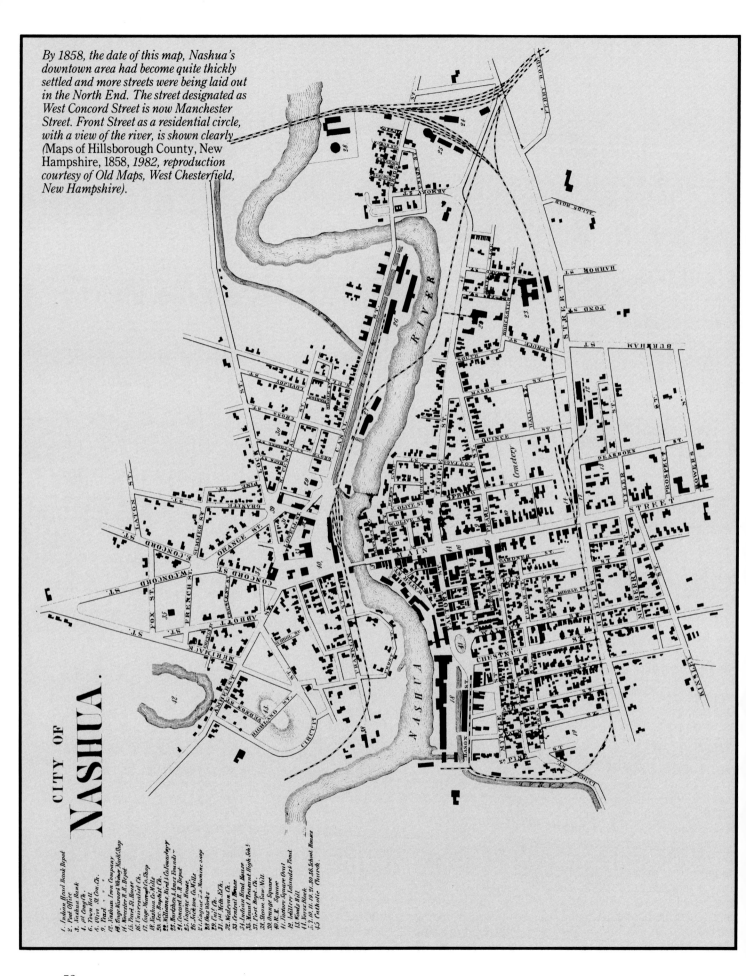

CITY OF
NASHUA.

1. *Indian Head Bank Depot*
2. *Post Office*
3. *Nashua Bank*
4. *1st Cong Ch.*
5. *Town Hall*
6. *West St. Con. Ch.*
9. *Pearl*
12. *Nashua Iron Company*
14. *Gage Warner & Whitney Mach. Shop*
15. *Worcester R. R. Depot*
15. *Pearl St. House*
16. *Universalist Ch.*
17. *Gage Warner Co. Shop*
18. *Nashua Co. Mills*
20. *2c. Baptist Ch.*
21. *Williams Bird & Co. foundry*
23. *Burleson & Ames foundry*
24. *Concord R. R. Depot*
24. *Crispus's Marine soap*
25. *Engine House*
26. *Gas Works*
29. *Cal. Ch.*
31. *1st Meth. Ch.*
32. *Wesleyan Ch.*
33. *Central House*
34. *Indian Head House*
35. *Mount Pleasant High Seat*
37. *First Bapt. Ch.*
38. *Stevens Saw Mill*
40. *R. K. Square*
40. *Orange Square*
41. *Fletcher Square Oval*
42. *Infantry Islands Pond*
44. *Woods Hill*
45. *Norris Block*
5, 7, 10, 11, 19, 21, 30, 36, School Houses
43. *Catholic Church*

52

This is one half of a stereopticon view of Auburn Street. The date is unknown but the street was laid out in the late 1850s. NPL file photograph

time when a potter's workshop stood there 150 years ago.

In 1885 mass transportation was introduced in a form that seems rather strange today. It was a horse railroad, complete with tracks. The system had a stable of twenty-four horses and ran six cars. After about ten years an electrified trolley system modernized the way people could get from one part of the city to another.

The culminating event of the eighties was the dedication of the Civil War Monument on October 15, 1889. One hundred years later, spotlighted at night, it serves as a focal point, recalling a desperate time in the country's history.

A huge increase in population was registered when the 1890 census results were tabulated. Nashua had grown by 44 percent over its previous census figure. By the turn of the century it would hit 23,000.

Several buildings stabbed the skyline during the energetic period of the nineties, creating vistas that are familiar today. In 1891 the Masons erected a building, Masonic Temple, at Main and East Pearl streets. This has been the home of the Nashua Trust Company since 1900. The following year the Odd Fellows put up the building at Main and Temple streets which, after renovation, has been rechristened the Landmark Building. The Whiting Building went up also in 1892 and by 1894 the tall tower of the First Church would be raised.

Nashua has had its share of scandals and bizarre happenings. Temptation and human frailty have manifested themselves here as everywhere. A story that had the whole town talking in the mid-nineties concerned the personable and popular ex-mayor, Frank McKean. He suddenly disappeared, with legal authorities in hot pursuit, when it was discovered that he had embezzled up to $90,000 from the bank where he was employed. It was a shock to people who knew him to learn that he had apparently been supporting a second household in Boston for many years. When Parker's *History of Nashua* came out, McKean's portrait and biography were conspicuously missing from the roster of leading public figures. McKean surfaced in a South American country where he died several years later. When his body was returned to Nashua for burial, the editor of the *Telegraph* commented on the tragedy, recalled what a likable and interesting chap McKean had been and suggested that he be forgiven for his failings.

In January 1901, Nashua observed the passing of what had been a tumultuous century and turned its face expectedly toward the changes ahead. As it began plans to celebrate its fiftieth anniversary of cityhood, there was an undercurrent of feeling that it had, after many struggles, reached a certain level of maturity, that the town had truly become a city.

A stereopticon view of Prospect Street gives a rather bleak impression, in spite of the substantial-looking houses, because trees had not had a chance to grow. This street, like Auburn, was first laid out in the late 1850s.
NPL file photograph

THE WASHINGTON HOUSE.

A sketch from an 1892 newspaper article affords a rare view of what the corner of Factory and Main streets looked like before 1853. It was in that year that the Washington House, shown at the left, was moved to a new location at Main and Bowers streets. The Washington House was built in 1830 by Thomas Chase who as a young man helped to clear the land where the first mill was built. Chase was a popular innkeeper and his hotel was a favorite gathering place, especially for military groups. When President Andrew Jackson came to Nashua in 1833, he had breakfast there.

Here is a sketch of the same building in 1883, the year in which it was destroyed by fire. At the time it was a furniture factory. Obviously, for use by various industries, it had undergone additions. In this second location at Bowers and Main streets, it was the home of the Nashua Watch Company, one of Nashua's most spectacular industrial failures. The Cardboard and Glazed Paper Company also used the building at one time during its history. At another time it was a shoe factory. The new Medical Building for Memorial Hospital is now on the site. (1883 Map of Nashua, published by Puritan Press 1982).

S. I. FOX, FURNITURE MANUFACTORY

The Progress of Nashua.

The progress of Nashua has not been so rapid as that of some of the neighboring cities, but it has been steady, healthy and ever onward. It has not retrograded in hardly any of the branches of business. Its manufacturing and mechanical prosperity was never at a higher point than at the present time. In both of these branches of material wealth a large amount of capital has been invested; and these enterprises have been remarkably well managed and have, consequently, been attended with decided success.

To show the progress Nashua has made and the changes which have taken place within the last fifteen years, it is only necessary to cite the following facts:—

In 1840, there were no buildings on Water street, except the residences of Messrs. Searles, Shepard and Lakeman and the old Mills house. Since then all of the shops, foundries, &c., on that street, have been built. At that time, on Main street, from High street to Pearl street, where is now a continuous block of Stores, and the Pearl St. House, stood only an old blacksmith shop and an old barn. On the site of the Pearl St. Church, and the residences of Dr. Hammond and Wm. D. Beasom, Esq., stood the American House. The Post Office was then in Hunts' Building, at the corner of Main and Factory streets; in 1841 it was removed to Atwood's building, opposite where it now is, and, in 1849, it was removed to its present position. In 1840, High street, at the head of Harrison and Clay streets, was known as Bank's Hill; it was cut down in 1846, but the old block remained, until the great fire, in 1856. On the site of Noyes Block stood the Washington House, which was removed, in 1853, to its present position, on what was formerly "the Pottery," so called. Nearly all the buildings on Pearl, Hollis and Vine streets, have been erected within the past fifteen years. The same may be said of the buildings erected on Woods' and "Gun House," Hill.

On the site of Union Block, stood the residences of Messrs. Mark A. Adams and Alvah Kimball. This part of the city being adapted for business, they removed to a more retired locality, to give place for the erection of this new and commodious block.

In 1842, the present City Hall was commenced, and finished in 1843. The land was purchased of the late Aaron F. Sawyer, Esq., on which stood his house and office, a lot of about 95 by 133 feet. It is constructed of brick on a very durable foundation of stone, with a basement of fine hammered granite. The ornaments and balconies, most-

ly from Grecian patterns, are of cast iron. The portico, 7 by 18 feet, is of iron on a base of granite. The building is 66 by 90 feet, and consists of the basement, first and second stories, and the attic. The basement is used for lobbies, &c.; first story contains the Aldermanic, Common Council, Police and Court Rooms. In the second story is the City Hall, 70 feet long, 63 feet wide, 24 feet high, with moveable seats, and will comfortably seat 1300 persons. There is, also, in this story, each side of the stairway, two small rooms adapted for offices. The attic 70 by 20 feet, was finished for the use of military companies. The height of the building, from the ground to the top of cupola, is about 100 feet. Cost $23,000. In 1854, the building was lighted with gas. Since then the Pennichuck water has been introduced.

The Post Office in this city was established sometime between April 1st and July 1st, 1803, and Gen. Noah Lovewell appointed postmaster. The office was opened in the tavern of Mr. Cummings Pollard, who was appointed assistant postmaster, and had charge of the office until 1811. Up to that time it was located in the tavern now occupied as a dwelling house by Reuben Godfrey. In 1811, the office was removed to the Harbor, and placed under the charge of Israel Hunt, who was appointed assistant postmaster, and in whose dwelling house it was stationed. After its removal to the latter place, it being located near the residence of Gen. Lovewell, he continued to superintend the duties of the office personally until his death. Upon his death, John M. Hunt, Esq., was appointed and commissioned in June, 1820. He established the office in the office of I. and J. M. Hunt, (at the Harbor,) where it remained until 1826, when it was removed to Hunts' building, (now occupied by Messrs. White & Hill, &c.,) Nashua Village, soon after the erection of the cotton mills. Mr. Hunt held the office until July, 1841, when Mr. J. A. Wheat was appointed, who removed it to Atwood's building. Mr. Wheat continued in the office until January, 1843, when Mr. David Philbrick was appointed in his stead. In July, 1845, Mr. C. P. Danforth succeeded Mr. Philbrick. In April, 1849, Mr. A. P. Hughes was appointed, and the office was then removed to its present position. In April, 1853, Mr. George Bowers succeeded Mr. Hughes, and is now the present postmaster and a grandson of Gen. Noah Lovewell, the first postmaster above mentioned. The receipt for the first quarterly balance of postage, for the quarter ending June 30, 1803, was only *twenty cents !!* For the quarter ending Sept. 30, 1805, the receipts had increased to *two dollars and eighty-seven cents*, yielding a commission for discharging the duties of the office of *eighty-six cents* per quarter, or *three dollars forty-four cents* per annum. The receipts now amount to *twelve hundred and ninety-one dollars and eleven*

Nashua town and city directories are an excellent source for basic information on who lived in town when and where; in many cases the resident's occupation is given. The early directories, however, lack the street section; this feature was not added until the early 1920s. The ads are not only amusing but provide many facts about companies, sometimes including an illustration of their product. The first directory was published in 1843. In the 1857 edition an essay on "The Progress of Nashua" appeared.

cents per quarter. Fifty-one years ago there was not a single letter or newspaper brought into this city by mail conveyance.

The present facilities for travelling, when compared with that of bygone days, have placed the expedition of the mails on a par with their advancement in amount of business and increase of revenue. In former times, it took two or three days to travel to Boston, now one can go and come in half a day and perform a great deal of business besides.

BLOCKS, BUILDINGS AND HALLS.

Atwood's Block, Main street, next to the Bridge.
Beasom's Building, cor. Main and Factory streets.
Beasom's Hall, in Beasom's Building.
Central Building, Main street, north of the Bridge.
City Hall, Main, between Park and Temple streets.
Eayrs' Block, cor. Main and Park streets.
Exchange Building, Main street.
Fisher's Block, cor. Main and Water streets.
Foster's Block, cor. Main and Fletcher streets.
Franklin Hall, in Depot Building.
Fuller's Block, cor. Main and High streets.
Graves' Building, cor. Main and Franklin streets.
Greeley's Block, Railroad Square.
Greeley's Building, cor. Main and Lowell sts.
Goodrich's Building, cor. Main and Water streets.
Harmony Hall, (Odd Fellows,) in Noyes Block.
Hunts' Building, cor. Main and Factory streets.
Indian Head Hall, in Indian Head Coffee House.
Long Block, Main street, opposite City Hall.
Masonic Hall, in Greeley's Block.
Noyes' Block, Main, between Factory and High sts.
Noyes' Buildings, between Pearl and High streets.
Parkinson's Building, cor. Main and Pearl streets.
Parkinson's Hall, in Parkinson's Building.
Railroad Block, Railroad Square.
Shepard's Block, Factory street.
Thayer's Building, cor. Main and Thayer's Court.
Union Block, cor. Factory and Washington sts.

The corner of Water and Main streets in the 1850s is depicted in this charming print. "City" on the sign at the right referred to the City Bookstore, operated by Henry Copp, the uncle of Eldridge J. Copp who wrote a book about his Civil War experiences. The freight vehicle on the left, because of its slatted sides, could have been carrying a flock of chickens. The picture was a product of the studio of J. Sidney Miller who is listed in a business directory as one of three "Ambrotype, Photograph and Daguerrean Artists" (From Maps of Hillsborough County, New Hampshire, 1858, 1982, reproduction courtesy of Old Maps, West Chesterfield, New Hampshire).

This is the Nashua High School building that was built in 1853 just south of where the Masonic Temple is now located. The very first high school was built on the Mt. Pleasant site by the town of Nashville in 1849. Two years later Nashua put up a high school building on West Pearl Street. Two years after that the school shown in the photo was put into operation, the upper floor being used for a high school that consisted of one big study room and two recitation rooms. After 1869 this school was the high school for the entire city. The first high school graduation was in 1859. NPL file photograph

Nashua.

The artist who executed this delightful sketch did not sign and date it. He has left a priceless memento of a summer morning as he looked southward from the tower of the old Mt. Pleasant School. The haying activity and the cows pasturing suggest how rural the North End was in spite of signs of industrial activity on the horizon. NPL file photograph

A group of mothers and children enjoy a summer day in the early 1870s. Across the street to the right is the Vale Mills, a small cotton-making concern that was in operation for a number of years on lower Main Street just below Lake Street. At the left is the Bowers House. This house had an interesting origin. Its builder, Jonathan Lovewell, used timbers from the church known as the "Bird Meetinghouse." NPL file photograph

This tree stood for many years at the junction of Temple and East Pearl. For some obscure reason the huge and much-loved old elm tree was called the "Jackson elm." When it eventually had to be cut down, Nashuans felt that they had lost a community symbol. The tree represents the many beautiful elms that grew along the streets before the blight that killed them off. NPL file photograph

The coming of the railroad was truly a revolutionary advance in transportation. Nashua was fortunately placed to benefit from this new technology. After the Boston and Lowell line was in operation, here is how people could travel from Boston to Nashua:

> The cars for these lines will leave the depot in Boston at 9 o'clock A.M. On the arrival at Lowell carriages will take the passengers free of charge immediately on board the steamer which will convey them to Nashua, N.H., where stages will be in readiness to take them forward. The passengers will dine on board the steamer while she is passing up the river.

New England Palladium for June 1835

By 1839 it was possible to go all the way by train. The illustration shows the kind of locomotive which would pull the cars. From Bradlee, The Boston and Lowell Railroad, the Nashua and Lowell Railroad and the Salem and Lowell Railroad.

LOCOMOTIVE "LION" NASHUA & LOWELL R. R. 1844

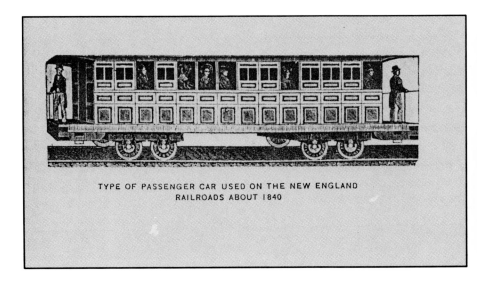

TYPE OF PASSENGER CAR USED ON THE NEW ENGLAND RAILROADS ABOUT 1840

Here was the state of the art in railroading by the seventies. The photo shows the roundhouse near Union Station. The locomotive was somewhat more complicated than the 1844 "Lion" but still depended on a wood fire to produce steam. By looking closely one can see the chunks of firewood in the tender. The roundhouse burned down in 1909. The photograph was taken by a Nashua photographer named Charles Lawrence.
NPL file

The farm of Zachariah Shattuck at Round Pond, off Amherst Street in the extreme northwestern corner of Nashua, was typical of the prosperous farms in outlying areas. Note how large and substantial the house was, with the usual attached barn. Shattuck's land holdings comprised four hundred acres.
Courtesy of Eleanor Balcom

The milkman was an institution that has now passed from the city streets. There was a time when homes depended on such a delivery service for a daily supply of fresh milk. This milk wagon was operated by the Shattuck farm—the sign reads "E. Z. Shattuck, Lic. 72."
Courtesy of Eleanor Balcom

The original First Baptist Church was on the same site as the old Baptist Church building of today. The entrance, however, was on Franklin Street. The church was built in 1833 and burned down in 1848 in a fire that spurred efforts for more efficient fire protection. The fire started in a business block that was called the Central Building where the New Hampshire Telegraph *had its office and printing press. Sketch from*
History of the First Baptist Church

The First Baptist Church that was built after the fire of 1848 looks imposing here in spite of the commercial places using its first floor space. McQuesten and Company, dealers in flour and grain, was in one corner while Blanchard and Currier,

Druggist and Apothecary, had the northern corner. This picture shows clearly the original steeple which was removed in 1920 because it seemed unstable.
Courtesy of Alfred Lawrence

This church was the home of the First Church from 1872, when it was built to replace the "Old Chocolate" which had been destroyed by fire, until 1894 when the congregation moved into the granite building at the top of Library Hill. As was customary, the ground floor was rented to retail establishments. The Free Will Baptists used the building for a few years, then it was home to various commercial firms; at one time it was a movie house, the Park Theater, and in its later days it was a hardware store. It burned down in 1967. The site was the corner of Pearson Avenue and Main Street.
NPL file photograph

The Episcopalians did not have an easy time establishing a parish in Nashua. St. Luke's Church, shown here, was the first church they erected; the location was at the junction of Temple and East Pearl streets. After struggling to keep it going during the 1860s the parish was declared extinct by the bishop of New Hampshire who encouraged the congregation to regroup. The movement to set up a new parish succeeded, culminating in the building of the present Church of the Good Shepherd in 1878.
NPL file photograph

The Church of the Good Shepherd, built by a Connecticut woman as a memorial to her daughter, is seen in a very early photo which also gives a perspective of what that part of Main Street was like at the time. NPL file photograph

1887

In 1887 a choir of young men and boys sang regularly at the Church of the Good Shepherd. William Nutting, later the founder of Nutting's Music Store, is third from the right in the front row. Courtesy of Blanche Nutting Bickford

Main Street Methodist Church was erected in 1868, making it the third oldest church building still in use. A turn-of-the century photo shows how the building looked with its original steeple and side entrance doors. The steeple, removed in 1946 because of danger from high winds, was replaced in very recent years. NPL file photograph

In this airbrushed photo of St. Louis de Gonzague Church, the church looks like an architect's model. It stood on West Hollis Street for over a hundred years. The whole city was shocked when it burned down one night in 1976. The bell tower was retained when the new church, quite modern in style, was put up on the same site.
Courtesy of Alfred Lawrence

The large wooden factory building known as the "Card Shop Building" is seen here a few years before it was displaced in the late thirties by the addition to the Telegraph Building. It was a familiar sight, fronting on Pearson Avenue, with its back to the river, from about 1850. The Cardboard and Glazed Paper Company occupied it for several years until the Franklin Street factory was built in the late 1880s.
NPL file photograph

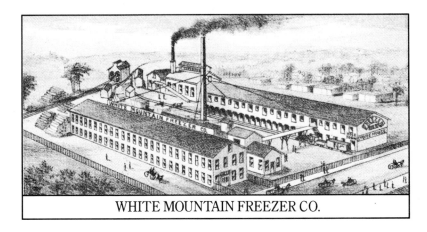

WHITE MOUNTAIN FREEZER CO.

Five important Nashua concerns are pictured here. These illustrations are from the fascinating panoramic map of Nashua in 1883, printed from the original lithograph by Puritan Press in 1982. At left is the White Mountain Freezer Company which was on East Hollis Street. The ice cream freezer, a household appliance that had to be cranked by hand, was invented by a Nashua man, Thomas Sands. Sands served a term as mayor in 1894.

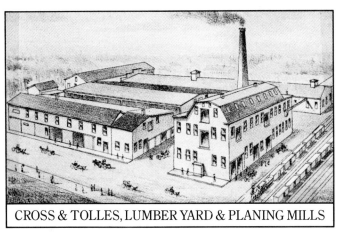

CROSS & TOLLES, LUMBER YARD & PLANING MILLS

GREGG & SON, DOOR SASH & BLIND, M.F.Y.

Above left the Cross and Tolles lumber yard is depicted. This old Nashua firm made a specialty of house finishings. James H. Tolles was mayor for three terms; Tolles Street in French Hill is named after him.

Above right is a sketch of Gregg and Sons lumber and wood products factory on Crown Street; this well-known firm was in business until the early 1960s.

At right is Eaton and Ayer, Bobbin and Shuttle works on Water Street. This company dated its operation back to the Baldwin bobbin-making business. The illustration shows what a busy industrial area Water Street was at one time.

EATON & AYER, BOBBIN & SHUTTLE WORKS

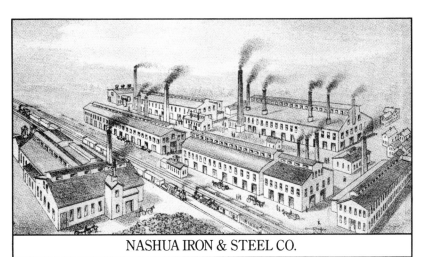

NASHUA IRON & STEEL CO.

The Nashua Iron and Steel Company, shown at left, was a leader in the production of steel forgings, nationally as well as locally. The sketch gives some idea of the extent of their many buildings in the East Hollis/Tyler streets area. Their mighty trip hammer, largest in the world for its time, was in the basement of what is now Osgood's Hardware Store. Their most famous products were the covers of the ports on the S.S. *Monitor* of Civil War days. The company dated its origins back to 1838, but it was no longer in business at the end of the century.

This illustration of the trip hammer of the Nashua Iron and Steel Company appeared in a National Geographic *publication,* America's Historylands.

Ingalls dated this photo as "about 1876." The fact that it was taken when the Tremont House still had its original portico suggests that a more likely date is around 1872, the year the Merchants Exchange was completed. The picture shows a street sprinkler that was used to help keep down the dustiness of unpaved streets in the summer.
NPL file photo

This photograph of the Merchants Exchange probably was taken around 1876 or after the Tremont House at left had acquired its porches. The window treatment of this building has always been one of its great beauties. The exact replicas that were installed during the current restoration contribute to the distinction of its "new look." The arcade was intended as a shelter from the weather for pedestrians. The weight of snow in the winters may have been a reason it was eventually removed. Jeremiah W. White, who built the block, had his own business at the north end.
Courtesy of Alfred Lawrence

This stereopticon view by a local photographer named Lovejoy shows the original Goodrich Block to good advantage. In the foreground materials are piled for the erection of the Phillips Block. The picture, therefore, can be dated about 1872.
NPL file photograph

A closeup of the Goodrich Block at the corner of Main and Water streets highlights the unique architectural features of this block that stood for over seventy years before it burned down in the 1920s. A new Nutting's Music Store building replaced it. Nutting's had been located on this site since about 1920 when William Nutting bought the block. Darrell's Music Store is now at this location.
NPL file photograph

The exact dating of many vintage photographs can be a matter for much friendly argument, but this one carries its own date: September 15, 1868. The "firemen's parade" is filled with life and activity here as bands from twelve towns meet in convention. The Laton Building in the background was new at the time.
NPL file photograph

A company selling stereopticon views offered about eighty with Nashua scenes as subjects. Most of these appear to have been taken in the 1880s. This picture of the oval at Railroad Square was entitled "Firemen's Parade." The large open space offered a good place for exhibits and drills by various organizations. The area looks rather bare and desolate here, however.
NPL file photograph

In this photo of Railroad Square and the top of Main Street, some cosmetic touches seem to have been given the oval. A street light has been put up and trees planted. The streetcar tracks at the bottom date the picture in the mid-nineties. Since the sign over the windows of the house at left says "Nashua House," it is safe to assume that a hotel was then at this site which over the years has seen several different small hotels. Billiards was offered in the Greeley Block to men who enjoyed this game. A harness manufacturer occupied the first floor. William Reed kept his grocery market in the Laton Building, with J. B. Parker's Real Estate office on the second floor. The photograph provides a clear idea of the original architecture of this building. *NPL file photograph*

A parade of some kind is coming down from the other side of the bridge but most pedestrians seem indifferent. The two men in the buggy may be a little impatient because traffic is temporarily tied up.

However, some ladies are interested enough to have climbed out a window in the Bowers Block to get a better view. NPL file photograph

This part of Main Street in the early eighties was a mix of residential and commercial buildings. The above view, taken on a winter day, probably a Sunday, shows the Noyes Block with the old Universalist Church on the left side of the photograph. Parking was simply a matter of finding a vacant hitching post for the horse. On some streets today the hitching posts are still in place in front of houses.
NPL file photograph

Col. George Bowers, the son of Jesse Bowers, was a great Nashua military hero. He fought with valor in both the Mexican and Civil wars. He is buried in the Old South Burying Ground.
Portrait from Parker's History of Nashua

This is a rare photograph of the Nutt's Building which stood in considerable architectural dignity at the corner of Park and Main streets from 1860 until it was destroyed by fire in 1959. The block was built by Charles C. Nutt, merchant and philanthropist. Nutt left a trust fund to benefit Memorial Hospital; this was used in 1957 to build the Nutt Surgical Wing. At the extreme left is a corner of the Nashua Literary Institute on Park Street. Courtesy of Robert Pinsonneault

This photo is famous for a strange reason—it was copied from the original stereopticon slide backward so that the two gentlemen chatting seemed to be on the wrong side of the street. It got printed several times that way. It is presented here as it appears on the slide, thus settling all arguments that the men were on the west side of Main Street, in front of the O. D. Murray house at number 221. Murray was a newspaperman who started the Oasis. He was also involved in the company that is now the Nashua Corporation. The time when the picture was taken was probably late 1870s. Note that a small boy seems to be waiting for Daddy to finish his conversation. The former Montgomery Ward building is now on the site of the Murray house.
NPL file photograph

It is a sleepy, perhaps hot afternoon in the
early 1880s in Abbott Square; when band-
stand concerts are given in the evenings,
the park and surrounding streets will come
alive with strolling crowds. A few years
later the Civil War Monument will be put
up. There are no automobile exhaust fumes
but a sanitation problem prevails because
of the many horses.
NPL file photograph

This was the way to go to the ball game in
the late 1880s or early 1890s when the bus
service was in the form of horse cars. A
question often asked is if this system required tracks—the answer is "yes." Tracks
made it much easier for the horses to pull
the cars. It was a fairly efficient, if not very
speedy, method of mass transportation.
The stables and parking spaces for the cars
were at the end of Kinsley Street.
NPL file photograph

George Underhill, founder of the Underhill Edge Tool Company, was called "the father of Crown Hill" because he bought a large tract of land in that area in the 1840s. On the highest point, which he called the "crown hill," he built the house shown in the photograph. With him in the buggy are his two sons, Karl and George, Jr. The photo is dated as around 1880. Courtesy of Mr. and Mrs. Richard Carson

Forty pupils seem like a large number for one teacher to superintend in a rural one-room schoolhouse. Perhaps she had an assistant who did not appear in the picture which was taken during the school year of 1885-1886. The school is identified as being in the south end of Nashua. The grandfather of the donor of this priceless group portrait was the little boy fourth from the left in the front row. There are undoubtedly other descendants of these children living in Nashua today. Courtesy of Alfred Lawrence

Military training at Nashua High School was started in 1887. Gen. Elbert Wheeler took an interest in initiating this program. This is the 1888 class of cadets at the Spring Street School. Standing are Capt. Samuel N. Hoyt, Lt. George W. Boutelle, Mus. Forrest W. Martin, Sgt. William Johnston, Pvt. Herman A. Osgood, Pvt. Freeman Marshall, Pvt. Frank E. Parker, Pvt. Charles M. Day, Pvt. Frank B. Howard, Sgt. Arthur G. Shattuck, Pvt. William Howe, Pvt. Harry M. Morse, Pvt. Joseph Ober, Pvt. Paul T. Norton, Pvt. Robert S. Wason, Pvt. Edward Lonergan, Principal James Willoughby, and Lt. Col. Jason E. Tolles, military instructor. Kneeling are Sgt. John Kimball, Corp. John B. Grover, Pvt. Ernest S. Woods, Pvt. Myron Mitchell, Pvt. Edward A. A. Dionne, Pvt. Arthur F. Cummings, Pvt. Frank R. Arnold, Pvt. Walter Williams, Corp. Fred W. Perkins, Corp. Charles H. Barker, Pvt. E. Ray Shaw, Corp. Harry Marshall, and Sgt. Walter B. Gage.
NPL file photograph

Burke's Bakery on Mulberry Street made home deliveries of crackers and other baked goods. The employees and management lined up for the photograph, along with two of the horses that pulled the wagons in the background. The following have been identified. From left to right, second through sixth, are William O'Neill, George Ellison, Mr. Landry, Freeman Herrick, and Charles A. Burke, the owner; eighth and ninth are Norman Boden and William Reid. Burke was mayor of Nashua in 1889 and 1890.
NPL file photograph

An 1888 picture could be called "Main Street, pre-Whiting Building." Photographs taken in this period reveal that the town was virtually strangling in festoons of electric wires going in all directions. The small building at right was called the Graves Building. It is summer and the Great Blizzard of the previous March has been forgotten.
Courtesy of Alfred Lawrence

Main Street, from Library, Nashua, N. H.

The same scene is shown here in a shot taken around 1903. It could be labelled "Main Street, post-Whiting Building." By this time the electric wiring system has been somewhat tidied up.
Courtesy of Alfred Lawrence

In addition to many other activities, such as inventions, Roswell T. Smith ran a bookstore in various locations from 1854 to 1891. The variety of things he sold, as suggested in his city directory ad, is apparent in the photograph. It must have been a browser's paradise! Throughout the nineteenth century after 1830 there were always several bookstores in town, many of which offered circulating library services. Magazines such as Leslie's Popular Monthly *and* Godey's Lady's Book *helped customers keep up with the hot topics of the day.*
NPL file photograph

It is regrettable that this photograph found its way into the collection with no identification. The name of the happy family is not known or where the house was located. It is presented as typical of middle class family life in the Nashua of the last century. The father stands proudly beside a status symbol, the horse and buggy. The three youngsters are on their best behavior but were undoubtedly as lively as children anywhere in any time. The female figure under the window may be an older daughter or a well-loved maiden aunt.
NPL file photograph

This was 76 Amherst Street in 1892 when the Putnam family was living there. It is another example of a typical middle class home of the period and the location. Note the ornamentation on the front porch pillars. The side porch covered with vines made a pleasant outdoor sitting room in hot weather.
NPL file photograph

The National Guard Armory at the corner of Canal and Grove streets was built in 1890. Mayor Charles Burke was so proud of the fact that it had been located in Nashua that he passed out photographs to his associates. Later a large addition was added to the west end. On February 3, 1957, it burned down in a spectacular fire.
NPL file photograph

LAYING CORNER STONE OF MASONIC TEMPLE, SEPTEMBER 14, 1889.

A placid photo of East Pearl Street opening off Main in 1876 suggests the residential character of this part of downtown before business buildings of several stories began to sprout on the scene.
NPL file photograph

This was the busy scene on the day in September 1889, when the Masonic lodges laid the cornerstone for the Masonic Temple. Among the items placed for posterity in the box was a copper plate taken from the cornerstone of the old Olive Street Meetinghouse when it was torn down in 1881. The inscription on the copper plate indicated that it had been placed there by the Grand Lodge of New Hampshire when it laid the cornerstone of the meetinghouse on October 24, 1825.
Courtesy of Robert Pinsonneault; photograph appears in Historical Sketch and Centennial Celebration of Rising Sun Lodge, *Cole, 1922*

79

Considerable research finally answered the question about the banner on the Greeley Building—"Join the L.A.W."—the initials stood for League of American Wheelmen. Lintott and Buswell's bicycle shop occupied the entire front space of the building at the time, the late nineties, so this connection makes sense.
NPL file photograph

Bicycling was a very popular sport in the latter part of the nineteenth century. In this well-known photograph, Ed and Willie Gilman, agents for the Columbia brand, look very serious as they show off their product.
NPL file photograph

The building that is the centerpiece of this photograph was built around 1866 when Nashua became the seat of Hillsborough County. It housed all of the county records and there was still room on the second floor for the library when it was first started. For most of its twentieth century existence the building was an annex to City Hall and was called the Municipal Records Building. Along with City Hall it was demolished in 1939. The city did not sell the narrow walkway on the north side of City Hall to the purchaser of these lots, and this lane cutting through from Main Street to Court Street next to the Nelson Building is still open.
NPL file photograph

NASHUA, N. H., WEDNESDAY, SEPT

AN OLD LANDMARK GONE.

The old building on Canal street, which is being torn down, was a landmark in Nashua. It was built about 1825, and its first occupants were Stiles & Tapley, carriage builders and painters, Franklin Foster, wheelwright, Hiram Baldwin, carriage maker, and the late Mark Gillis, carriage painter; there was also a blacksmith shop in the basement, on the south side, the ground being ten feet lower before the railroad was built and the building being three stories on that side. Mr. P. W. Prescott, father of Dr. R. B. Prescott, also had a harness shop in the building and died there, at his bench, suddenly, of paralysis in 1851. The building was widened about 1850 by the addition of 16 feet on the south side. The second story on the Canal street side was the home for many years of the NASHUA WEEKLY TELEGRAPH. It was afterwards occupied by S. S. Davis as a box shop. I. O. Woodward & Cory were occupants of the building 18 years, and among the other occupants were Frank D. Laton, Chicago dressed beef, Williams Hall, the latter using the east end for a storehouse. It had become a rookery and was a give away of Nashua to strangers who came into the city by the Boston & Lowell railroad. The improvement that is being made will be appreciated. *Torn Down - Oct. 1891.*

It is easy to date this picture of what later
became known as Library Hill. The First
Church, shown under construction in the
background, was built between May 1893,
and May 1894.
NPL file photograph

The First Church has been finished—
somehow its magnificence is in sharp
contrast to the dowdiness of neighboring
buildings. This incongruity would be
resolved a few years later when the Hunt
Building went up, its architects carefully
placing it so that it would harmonize with
the lines of the church.
NPL file photograph

It is not known what the occasion was for
this military gathering in front of City
Hall. From the ladies' costumes one would
guess that the time was the mid-nineties.
The local militia used the attic of City Hall
for meetings and drills. At the left of the
picture is Aaron Sawyer's law office and
house where, in a few years, the Nelson
Building would be erected.
Courtesy of the Peterborough
Historical Society

The Greeley House on Front Street still makes an enchanting picture from Main Street Bridge. The house is almost 150 years old, the last remnant of a residential area that was a little off the beaten track. The man who built it, Joseph Greeley, was not related to others of the same name in Nashua. His family was located in Hudson. His business interests appear to have been mostly in Concord. The view from the bridge would not be the same if it weren't there.
NPL file photograph

This is the corner of Pearson Avenue and Main, time probably the mid-nineties. Woodward and Cory were harness manufacturers. The laundry was on the Pearson Avenue side of the Sargent building, hence the conspicuous sign strung across the street, perhaps suggesting laundry hung out to dry.
Courtesy of Alfred Lawrence

Frank Ingalls, with his penchant for getting up to high places for unusual photographic angles, must have taken this overview from the First Church tower. The result is a wintry scene that could have been a set for a movie about a small New England city at the turn of the century.
Courtesy of Alfred Lawrence

83

There is such a traffic jam here that it must have been a Saturday when this photo was taken. Many farmers would be coming in to town to sell produce and do shopping. The photo conveys a feeling of a busy, prosperous community that was quite pleasant to live and work in.
Courtesy of Alfred Lawrence

Ingalls preserved this picture and gave an exact date—May 7, 1898. The unknown photographer who snapped it caught a dramatic moment as Company C, en route to the railroad station during the Spanish-American War, marched down East Pearl Street. The young boys probably wished that they were going too. Actually Nashua soldiers saw very little action in this war; most of them became ill in southern training camps.
NPL file photograph

The old veterans lead the young recruits going to yet another war in this scene in the spring of 1898. The John G. Foster Post No. 7, Grand Army of the Republic, escorts Company C to the train that will take them for service in the Spanish-American War.
NPL file photograph

Here is Canal Street at the intersection of Chandler, when there really was a canal running parallel to it. Company housing is on the other side of the street.
Courtesy of Alfred Lawrence

At first glance this picture may give the impression that both the police and the National Guard had been called out to control the crowd trying to "slaughter the stock" at Floyd's fire and water sale. Actually the occasion was a reception for visiting military dignitaries at the time of the Spanish-American War.
NPL file photograph

This rural schoolhouse was on the Milford Road. This was probably only part of the student body that attended the school. The donor of the photo gives the date as "about 1893" and says that one of the girls married into her husband's family. The porch, an unusual feature on schoolhouses, made a good place to locate the flag pole.
Courtesy of Eleanor Balcom

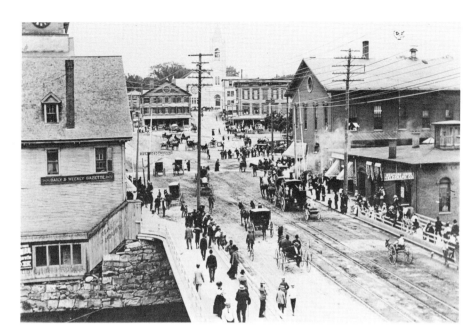

It is quarter past eleven on a morning in the mid-1890s when a parade has just ended and participants are dispersing in Railroad Square. The young boys driving their donkey carts behind the steam calliope give a whimsical touch to the scene—they must have been having so much fun! NPL file photograph

Ingalls, shooting from the top of the mill-yard chimney in 1900, aimed his camera northwesterly. Beyond the bend in the river one can make out the extent of devel-opment and also the large amount of still-vacant land. NPL file photograph

A 1900 view of the millyard when there were bridges across the canal for foot traffic. The steps in right foreground led down to the wheelhouse which may still be seen today, with most of the machinery in place. Courtesy of Alfred Lawrence

In this winter scene can be seen the railroad line that was an important artery for the cotton mill, bringing in raw material and distributing the finished goods.

During the 1915 strike workers tried to stop the freight trains from coming into the millyard.
Courtesy of Alfred Lawrence

This is another Ingalls photo taken from the top of the millyard chimney in 1900. Examined closely, many features can be discerned quite clearly: the Odd Fellows Building, center left; Main Street Methodist Church steeple; St. Louis de Gonzague Church steeple at right center. Note the vacant lot at the eastern end of the mill buildings—Mill No. 7 had not yet been erected there.
Courtesy of Alfred Lawrence

The employees of Proctor Brothers, the lumber company, gathered for a group portrait one day in 1899. Their consciousness of the formality of the occasion was indicated by the donning of hats. One way of looking at the picture, therefore, is as a study in styles of men's hats and the various ways in which they could be worn!
NPL file photograph

There are comparatively few photographs available showing the operations of the local cotton mills. In this one a spinner tends her machine. She was probably French-Canadian, helping to support a family that included several children. The yarn she was spinning may have gone into the blankets that the Nashua Manufacturing Company produced.
Courtesy of Alfred Lawrence

Adm. George Dewey occasionally visited Nashua to see his sister, Mary Dewey Greeley, the wife of Dr. George Greeley. On one such visit he was persuaded to appear in a parade. Here are two pictures snapped by an observer when the parade was passing the corner of Main and West Hollis streets. The buildings in the background were the Spalding Building and the grain elevator and farm supply store of O. B. Tilson. Courtesy of Mrs. James Walsh of Fairfield, Connecticut

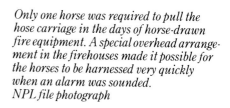
Only one horse was required to pull the hose carriage in the days of horse-drawn fire equipment. A special overhead arrangement in the firehouses made it possible for the horses to be harnessed very quickly when an alarm was sounded.
NPL file photograph

The Amherst Street Fire Station is the oldest now in operation. It was built in 1893. Two of the firemen enjoy the spring sunshine in this photo, probably taken soon after the station was built.
Courtesy of Alfred Lawrence

Under winter conditions fire equipment was put on runners for speedier response to alarms. Central Fire Station was erected in 1870 after a previous station on the same site had burned down. It is now the Nashua Center for the Arts.
NPL file photograph

This familiar photograph is one of the most popular historical pictures because of the human interest inherent in the companionship of the fireman, George Osborn, and his dog. The dog was not just a pet or mascot—it performed a real role in the work of the fire department by detecting the location of people in burning buildings so that they could be rescued.
NPL file photograph

Here can be seen the physical evidence that Nashua at the turn of the century was very much a railroad center. St. Francis Xavier Church, seen in the upper left, had been built in 1896 on Chandler Street and could be seen from almost any point.
Courtesy of Paul Newman, from his postcard collection

Ingalls climbed to the tower of St. Francis Xavier Church to capture these views of French Hill. He was shooting north up Chandler Street. In the first photograph a sculptured detail of the tower can be seen at lower left. The shedlike buildings behind the tenements on the right were undoubtedly outhouses which served as handy places for the housewives to attach one end of their clotheslines.
NPL file photograph

In the second photograph Chandler Street is at the left, with Whitney Street intersecting at the right. Older people who lived in the area as children remember playing on the sand pit. These pictures demonstrate the great sociological value of the camera in recording environments in the lives of ordinary people.
NPL file photograph

In 1891 a police station was built on Court Street behind City Hall. This was a facility that was badly needed to relieve congested space in the main municipal building. The photo shows how it looked around 1920. After headquarters for the Police Depart- *ment was provided as part of the new City Hall, the building was bought by the Coffey Post, American Legion. It is still owned by this organization.*
Courtesy of Don Hamel

The Spence Dry Goods Company had a
flourishing department store in the Noyes
Building for about twenty years. Samuel
Spence came to Nashua in 1894 and
started this store which at one time employed a staff of twenty-four. The shirt-
waist style of dress worn by the salesladies
in the photograph dates it as late nineties.
Many women worked in such retail establishments as well as in dressmakers'
workshops, millinery stores, and other
businesses.
Courtesy of Jean Carson

D. C. Cheever had this picture taken by a
New York photographer who specialized in
commercial work; it was probably intended
to be used in advertising his millinery shop
on Main Street across from Pearson
Avenue. This was a period when hats as
fashion accessories were taken very serious-
ly. The camera also recorded a dim picture
of the church on the other side of the street
reflected in the window.
NPL file photograph

Arthur W. Phelps's house was directly across the street from the Chandler residence. The site is now part of Memorial Hospital's holdings. Phelps was a son of George Phelps who came to Nashua in 1870 and was in the coal business. He went into business with his father. The house is a good example of the substantial residences in this part of town.
Courtesy of Alfred Lawrence

The Romanesque Revival style architecture of the Odd Fellows Building (now the Landmark Building) is illustrated in this detail. After the Masons had put up their Temple at East Pearl and Main streets, the Odd Fellows bought up the property of the Colburn family at Temple and Main and by 1892 had dedicated their own tall building.
Courtesy of Jeannine Levesque

George Stark, 1823-1892—the man and his house. Stark was a grandson of Maj. Gen. John Stark, the hero of the battle of Bennington. At an early age he was employed in helping the engineers who laid out the Nashua and Lowell Railroad. He worked on several railroads before becoming manager of the Boston and Lowell line in 1857. The portrait is an engraving. NPL file

Parker's history made this comment on the beautiful house Stark built in the early 1850s at the junction of Manchester and Concord streets: "His family residence at Nashua, though showing no taste for ostentation or display, is an elegant structure in the villa style, furnished with every comfort and convenience and adorned with works of art." The house is now on the National Register of Historic Places. For many years it was owned by the Christian Science Church. It is presently a private office building. The attractive small park where the Firemens' Memorial stands was given to the city by Stark. NPL file photograph

ALBIN BEARD.

Albin Beard, 1808-1862, was a man for all time. When his twin brother, Alfred, died in 1839, he took over the editorship of the New Hampshire Telegraph *and was one of its greatest editors. Beard was a leading advocate of reunification of the two towns into the city of Nashua and served a term as mayor. He had a strong sense of humor and would undoubtedly be amused as well as amazed at the changes that have taken place in the Nashua that he loved during the 125 years since his death. Beard was very musical and conducted the choir of the Unitarian Church. Photograph from Parker's* History of Nashua

Roswell T. Smith, 1825-1901, substituting a crutch for the leg he could not walk on, lived life fully—traveling, inventing, and engaging in several business enterprises. On his passing he was deeply mourned by the entire community. NPL file photograph

97

Jesse Bowers, 1785-1854, came here as a young man from Chelmsford. He married Gen. Noah Lovewell's daughter, Betsy, and lived in the Lovewell house on lower Main Street; the house is often also referred to as the Bowers House. Bowers was very active in town affairs and served for many years in the state legislature, including several terms as a state senator. He was the father of Col. George Bowers, the military hero.
NPL file photograph

Virgil C. Gilman, 1827-1903, contributed in many ways to the growth and improvement of his city. He was a member of the original group that started what is now the Nashua Corporation. He was a director in several banking and industrial enterprises and was greatly interested in agriculture, helping to develop the Plymouth Rock fowl. Gilman also helped to start the fish hatchery. He was mayor in 1865 and served on the Board of Education and the Library Board of Trustees.
NPL file photograph

Prof. David Crosby, 1808-1881, directed the Nashua Literary Institute, an excellent private high school, for almost forty years. Parker's History of Nashua *described his final days: "Although unable to see, he instructed classes at his home on Church Street, making from memory the most minute and careful explanations. He followed this work till five or six weeks before his death. It may thus be said that he died in harness, in the work of a profession he had honored." Crosby was assisted in the school by his wife, Louisa Hunton Crosby, who was his equal as a teacher.*
A Glenton photograph; NPL file

Dr. George P. Greeley, 1833-1892, was a member of the Greeley family that built the brick building on Railroad Square. He was born in the Greeley house on Amherst Street. His wife was Mary P. Dewey of Montpelier, Vermont, a sister of Adm. George Dewey. Dr. Greeley was highly regarded in his profession but was a well-rounded man in other areas. He is described as being "thoroughly informed in literature and history."
NPL file photograph

Anne Mason Morrill. ?-1875, was Mrs. Hiram T. Morrill. Women were undeniably important in the cultural and social life of Nashua in this era. Unfortunately their activities and achievements were eclipsed by the publicity about their husbands. Mrs. Morrill, who lived on Orange Street, was originally from Boston. She was descended from Gen. Henry Woods, a pioneer of

Groton. Her husband was the Civil War mayor and she shared in the special sacrifices and duties that fell to him at that time. Parker's history praised her "for noble deeds as wife, mother and neighbor." Her grandson, James H. Fassett, became superintendent of schools and wrote a history of Nashua for children.
NPL file photograph

The Nashua Photo Company, which had its studio at 103 Main Street, did this photographic study of a blacksmith shop. Blacksmithing was an important field of work when horses were a chief means of transportation. There was even a blacksmiths' union organized in Nashua. NPL file photograph

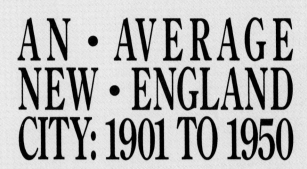

4

AN · AVERAGE
NEW · ENGLAND
CITY: 1901 TO 1950

In March 1901, the Library Board of Trustees was finally given the go-ahead to start work on their new building. Two and a half years later, the Hunt Memorial Building was opened for inspection by the public. There was no formal dedication ceremony. The construction of the library had left a trail of bitter feelings that no amount of oratory could have obliterated.

When Mrs. Mary A. Hunt and Miss Mary E. Hunt in 1892 presented the city with $50,000 to build a library in memory of John M. Hunt, they had no idea what a tempest they were initiating. At one point, the disappointed women actually asked for their money back.

The problem concerned the selection of a suitable site by the city. North End/South End jealousies of half a century before came to the surface as disagreements raged within City Hall and on the streets. The site favored by many was the very one where the library would be eventually constructed—the Greeley lot on Railroad Square. Because of the conflicting opinions, however, there was a fatal delay in laying claim to this choice piece of land and in the meanwhile a syndicate of speculators bought up the property. The matter came before the New Hampshire Supreme Court three times before the city finally took the land by eminent domain. There was still further delay because of a problem involving the investment of the gift money, the city insisting that the fund must be built up again before building could start.

Trick photography around 1900 produced this unique shot of four important buildings. From left to right are the Nashua City Hall, the County Records Building, the Odd Fellows Building, and the Telegraph Block. The only one that is still part of the downtown scene is the Odd Fellows which has been appropriately renamed "the Landmark Building." Courtesy of Paul Newman, from his postcard collection

The commercial buildings on the site were cleared away; the brick Greeley Block that had stood there for almost seventy years was moved across to Clinton Street. The Boston architectural firm of Cram, Goodhue and Ferguson submitted the design that the trustees liked best. Ralph Adams Cram was a member of this firm and the Gothic building still standing today embodies many of his ideas. Now on the National Register of Historic Places, the Hunt Memorial Building is a cherished landmark. After the library itself moved to its new building on Court Street in 1971, it was renovated to serve as the administrative offices of the Nashua school system.

A man who had been brought up in Nashua had been away for many years. When he finally made a return visit, he could not believe the changes in the old Nashua that he remembered. He recalled the many pleasant hours he had spent at the library as a student and headed up Library Hill. As he stood in front of the Hunt Building he thought "Thank heavens, here is one place that has not changed!" It was quite a shock when he entered and learned otherwise.

Nashua in the first half of the twentieth century can probably best be described as an average New England city for its size. The population grew slowly but steadily, achieving a 50 percent increase between 1900 and 1950. Several different ethnic groups contributed to this growth. Successive waves of French-Canadian migration plus the high birth rate of this group resulted in Nashua being half French by the end of the period. During the 1890s and the early years of the twentieth century, many Greek, Polish, Lithuanian, and Jewish immigrants came

here to settle and raise families. The Irish, who had started to come to the area before the Civil War, accounted for a fairly large proportion of the population.

Basically, a fairly cohesive social structure had carried over from preceding decades, a well-understood way of life that was distinctively "Nashuan." Through two world wars, labor troubles, a depression, a fire that destroyed almost one-fourth of the city, a disastrous flood, this inherited sense of community served as a force for unity. The ethnic groups were assimilated with surprisingly little friction. The necessary adjustments to changes that came with the times were taken in stride.

Although characterized as "average," meaning typical middle America, it was by no means a stagnant community. It was constantly building bigger and better facilities to replace the old and outmoded. It was always expanding, modernizing, and improving services to its citizens.

Two other public buildings that were erected in the first decade of this century were the Post Office and the Courthouse. By 1906 Nashua had its first separate post office building, a classically beautiful structure that graced Court Street for many years.

The second decade saw the long-awaited new city charter put into effect. It did away with two-body city government, set up the present Aldermanic Board, and changed the mayor's term to two years. Women took immediate advantage of the fact that it enabled them at last to vote for members of the Board of Education; they elected Ruth French to the Board in 1914.

In 1915 a strike at the cotton mills resulted in vio-

The Whiting Block had probably been standing for about ten years when this photo was taken. It was the home of the Indian Head Bank from 1893 until 1909 when the bank moved into the Telegraph Block. The bank, founded in 1851, previously had its offices in the Central House and the depot building. The Franklin Street corner basement area was a restaurant, described by the sign in the window as "First Class." William H. Reed had his grocery story at the north corner. Next door was the Commercial Inn. In recent years the building has been completely renovated. Courtesy of Alfred Lawrence

lence that caused the death of one worker and injuries to several. In 1916 the two big companies, Nashua Manufacturing and Jackson, officially merged operations under one management.

The aftermath of World War I was a critical time as the influenza epidemic struck Nashua; thousands were ill, taxing all medical resources, and many died from the severity of the disease.

Nashua in the twenties was caught up in the pervading atmosphere of that exuberant decade. Prohibition produced the same problems that were experienced all over the country. Stills in town were raided and in one ludicrous incident an undertaker's hearse was searched on a tip that it was being used for rum-running. The local baseball club was called the Millionaires, perhaps reflecting the general aura of self-confident prosperity.

Here are some "firsts" for the twenties: the first Rotary Club started in 1921; the Nashua Symphony Orchestra formed in 1923; Nashua Chamber of Commerce be-

gan in 1926; and Community Chest inaugurated in 1929 with Sceva Speare as its first president.

Two bank buildings were built at about the same time during this period. After a terrible fire destroyed the Telegraph Block, the Indian Head Bank rebuilt on the same site. The Second National Bank tore down the old Tremont House and erected the building that now houses the Bank of New Hampshire.

On May 4, 1930, a very windy Sunday, fire broke out under a railroad trestle and spread rapidly, soon engulfing the entire Crown Hill section. Within a few hours it had caused $2.5 million damage to homes and businesses. Infant Jesus Church was one of the casualties. The relief organization that immediately marshalled all available resources was extremely efficient and the area, which looked as if a bomb had hit it, made a remarkable recovery. Within a year most of the houses had been rebuilt. Four hundred families had been burned out, many of them losing everything they owned.

The serenity of bright sunshine illuminates this view of Main Street looking south, taken at 4:15 in the afternoon sometime in the early part of the century. Although an automobile is parked in front of the railroad station, horse-drawn vehicles dominate the traffic.
Courtesy of Nancy Atherton Buell

During the thirties a spirit of "boosterism" prevailed, as indicated by the erection of an actual gate at the state line. The city proclaimed itself "the Gate City to New Hampshire," welcoming travelers who were heading north. A log cabin information booth was set up in Railroad Square to emphasize this role.

It had been obvious for some time that the old City Hall was beyond repair and that a new center for the city government was needed. Federal assistance under the WPA program was obtained to make this a reality. A new high school was also built with federal funds helping to foot the bill; the first class to graduate from it was in 1938. This building is now the Elm Street Junior High School.

During the forties the community demonstrated great unity of purpose in the war effort. At one time it was estimated that 13 percent of the population was in the various services. War casualties numbered 103 men and women who gave their lives in World War II.

The biggest casualty of the postwar period was the cotton industry. The company that for 125 years had provided jobs for thousands of people sold out to Textron, Inc., which by 1948 decided it was not profitable to keep the mills in operation. On September 13 the announcement was made to a stunned city that the mills were closing down. The Era of Cotton had come to an end!

The remarkable story of the Nashua-New Hampshire Foundation and its leadership in bringing Nashua out of this crisis is being told in detail in another publication. It is enough to say here that the city's response, its resilient spirit attracted national media attention. One newspaper commented on the "miracle of how Nashua, New Hampshire, threatened a year ago with the loss of its major industry and mass unemployment, became—not a ghost town—but a bright spot in New England's employment picture."

The Hunt Memorial Building was still under construction when this picture was taken. The clock was purchased by public subscription. The Greeley Building is shown on its new location on Clinton Street; later a fourth story was added when it became a hotel.
NPL file photograph

The influence of Ralph Adams Cram's school of architecture is demonstrated in the Gothic entrance of the Hunt Building. The original heavy oak doors emphasized this cathedral-like effect. The pedestals on either side were probably intended to hold statues but this detail was never carried out.
NPL file photograph

The Reading Room of the Hunt Library in 1907 probably looked much the same as when it opened in 1903. By the time the library moved out in 1971, all of the wall space was covered by bookcases, even in front of the fireplace. A microfilm machine stood at the far end and a copying machine was in constant use near the doorway. Photo by A. H. Seifert; NPL file

The back wing of the Hunt Library was originally the Children's Room. The impression in this photo is decidedly cheerless, in fact one can't help wondering if little girls without hats were refused entrance! Later a sunny space downstairs was turned into the Children's Department. A well-known artist painted a mural on the walls depicting in glowing colors all the wildflowers of New Hampshire. The back wing for a while was called the New Hampshire Room—a plaque mounted by the DAR to this effect is still in place. NPL file photograph

This was the farm of Joseph Thornton Greeley who in 1881 bequeathed it to the city as a potential site for a public park. It took almost thirty years for this idea to become a reality. Many civic-minded citizens, especially John E. Cotton, helped to procure additional land so that the park would extend through to Manchester Street. NPL file photograph

In 1911 John E. Cotton gave additional money to build the Rest House for the park. Here we see it when under construction.
Courtesy of Alfred Lawrence

Clara Roby Wheeler, Gen. Elbert Wheeler's wife, gave a drinking trough to be installed at Greeley Park. It is still there although it had to be moved out of the way of modern traffic. Here we see Mrs. Wheeler giving her own horse a drink.
Courtesy of Margaret Beasom Swart

There is poetry in this exhilerating photo of trees at Greeley Park. Unfortunately this particular grove was badly damaged in the 1938 hurricane. However, there are still many fine trees in the park which consists of 125 acres of land. Nashua is fortunate to have this green breathing space in the middle of the city. The town should be grateful that John Cotton and others gave funds to make it a reality. Many people take advantage of the outdoor fireplaces for picnics in the summer. The spacious lawns are used for all kinds of events. Development of the park may have taken a long while but it was worth waiting for.
NPL file photograph

Dr. Ella Blaylock Atherton, Nashua's famous woman doctor, is shown here in a formal portrait with her husband, Capt. Henry B. Atherton. Their romance was an unusual one. She had been a practicing physician for several years when she married the Civil War veteran who was a widower with grown children. They had two sons, one of whom was Blaylock Atherton, well-known Nashua lawyer and state legislator. Dr. Ella, a Canadian by birth, outlived her husband by many years. Courtesy of Nancy Atherton Buell and Janet Atherton Snow, their granddaughters

In this winter scene on Fairmount Street, the Atherton house looks as solidly rooted as if it had always stood there. Actually the house represents the most famous house-moving incident in Nashua history. Capt. Henry Atherton could not bear to see the Spalding House on Temple Street torn down to make way for the Courthouse. He bought the house for a very small amount of money and moved it all the way up Main Street and on to its present setting. The barn was also moved; it had at one time been the barn for Isaac Spalding's house. Courtesy of Nancy Atherton Buell

Sometimes an imperfect photo, taken with a simple camera of an earlier period, can still convey a slice of life frozen in time. Such a cameo is this shot of Dr. Ella Blaylock Atherton, shown (center) admiring a friend's new touring car in the summer of 1909. She is surrounded by family members, including her two young sons and her housekeeper, Jessie McLaren (right).
Courtesy of Nancy Atherton Buell

Ira Harris, bank cashier and active community member, took this picture from the south end of the Main Street bridge, looking west, on a very still day. The reflection in the river is so perfect that only the sign on the building at right indicates which side is up. Caleb Marshall had a wholesale produce business on Franklin Street for many years in the early part of the century.
From a Harris family album at NPL

*On Concord Street after a big blizzard the
important plowing operation was clearing
a way for the trolleys.
Courtesy of Alfred Lawrence*

The trolley arrives on schedule in Abbott Square in spite of the drifts. The photo was taken during the period when the Abbot House (facing, at left) had been altered by an addition with a tower on its front. A later owner, William Spalding, wisely removed this excrescence and restored the house to its original classic appearance. NPL file photograph

Dr. George A. Underhill was a physician who was also a pharmacist. The Underhill Drug Company was on this corner of the Merchants Exchange Block from 1903 until 1912 when Underhill died. Note the mortar and pestle prominently hung on the building.
Courtesy of Paul Newman, from his postcard collection

In this formal portrait, taken by the Nashua Photo Company, Mrs. Helen Bell Underhill, wife of Dr. George Underhill, poses in an intricately embroidered gown typical of the fashions of the Edwardian period.
Courtesy of Jean Carson, a descendant of the Underhill family

The Nashua Daily Press *was started to fill the void left when the old* Nashua Gazette *stopped publishing in 1895. By 1905 the* Press *also had folded up. As seen here, it was printed in the Parkinson Building at the corner of West Pearl and Main. This building, now the site of Miller's, had been on the corner for almost a century when it burned down on October 4, 1948.*
NPL file photograph

Kinsley Street, Nashua, N. H.

The Chandler House, now the Chandler Library and Ethnic Center, is shown with an ornamental fence around it. This neighborhood scene exudes so much tranquillity that one can almost hear the clang of the trolley as it approaches the turn into Main Street.
Courtesy of Paul Newman,
from his postcard collection

*Nashua City Station is shown here at an unusual angle—most photos were taken from the Main Street side. The station was built in 1848 although the location had been used for passengers and freight from the time railroad service had been started.
Courtesy of Paul Newman,
from his postcard collection*

The only reason an amateur photographer would go out in a snowstorm to take pictures has to be experimentation. The figure at the right appears to be a companion holding a device to light the scene. The N. H. Banking Company began in 1880 and was located in the corner of City Station for several years. It was one of the first guaranty savings banks in the state. The curious photographer was Ira Harris and the print was found in his album at NPL.

*The first synagogue of Temple Beth Abraham was at the corner of Cross and Locke streets. It was erected around 1902 when there were about thirty Jewish families living in town. In 1969 this community built a new synagogue on Raymond Street.
Courtesy of Nancy Atherton Buell*

116

Highland Spring Sanatorium, Nashua, N. H. For Nervous Invalids.-A. E. Brownrigg, M. D. Sup't

The Highland Spring Sanatorium, managed by Dr. E. A. Brownrigg, was located at Beauview Avenue and Manchester Street. Dr. Brownrigg was a psychiatrist who came to Nashua in 1898. He opened the sanatorium around 1900 as an institution where patients with nervous disorders could be treated. After an interruption while he served as a major in the medical corps during World War I, he returned to Nashua and reopened the sanatorium which he continued to operate until about 1928. In the last few years of his life he served on the Veterans' Bureau which sent him to several veterans' hospitals. Dr. Brownrigg died in Wyoming in 1933.
Courtesy of Paul Newman,
from his postcard collection

Employees and management of the Nashua Baking Company had their picture taken in 1932. All the workers at this bakery were French. Their specialty was Country Club bread. They went into business in 1910 as successors to Gaudette, Joron and Levesque. The location was Elm and Mulberry streets in a building that is still standing. The company went out of business in the early forties.
Courtesy of Renée Dube

The Shattuck Street Elementary School was built in 1908 and ceased to be a public school in 1963. The building since then has been used for various education-related and social service activities. It is presently the home of the Greater Nashua Child Care Center.
Courtesy of Nancy Atherton Buell

117

The Harbor School was the elementary school originally on Lake Street. It was torn down around 1924 and replaced with the brick James B. Crowley School, named after the mayor who served several terms during the World War I period.
Courtesy of Nancy Atherton Buell

The postcards bearing these two views are postmarked 1906 but the photos may have been taken somewhat earlier. The designation, "Tremont Square," came into use for this intersection when it became the terminus for out-of-town trolleys. In the "north" perspective the Howard Building can be seen in the distance, giving that end of Main Street a graceful curve. The small boy seems to be filling a jug from the trough. The box on legs, with attendant in a nearby chair, was either a popcorn or roast peanut machine.
Courtesy of Paul Newman, from his postcard collection

Tremont Square, North, Nashua, N. H.

The "south" view shows several horse-drawn vehicles. By 1906 there were seventy autos in town and the absence of even one or two supports the feeling that the photos were made a few years earlier. It is interesting to note that the row of trees down the middle of Main Street in front of the Tremont House and the Merchants Exchange has disappeared. They probably interfered with passengers getting on and off the trolleys.
Courtesy of Paul Newman, from his postcard collection

Tremont Square, South, Nashua, N. H.

A big step forward in transportation was the establishment of an electric trolley system. In 1894 the Lowell and Suburban Street Railway Company gained control of the trolley lines in Nashua and set up an electrified system that ran from Lowell to Nashua. The trolleys made it possible for people to make trips outside town. Lakeview, a park near Lowell, was within reach and a day's outing at Canobie Lake became a common recreational event. Electric cars in Nashua had been phased out by 1931. NPL file photograph

Colonial Theatre, Nashua, N. H.

The Colonial Theater was an entertainment center and movie house from 1911 until 1954. It was located just south of the Masonic Temple, using the walls of the old high school building. Stores were built in front of it and the entrance to the theater was through the arcade shown on the right. During the peak period when movies were a chief attraction for amusement, before television, there were as many as five theaters regularly showing films. Courtesy of Paul Newman, from his postcard collection

The Nelson Department Stores erected the building, still called the Nelson Block, in 1904. The Sawyer House that it displaced was the last residential holdout in this section of Main Street. Considerable care and expense was taken to give the exterior a look of tasteful distinction. Recent renovations have enhanced these features, while modernizing it in tune with the downtown of today which is moving toward more office space and less retail. The top of this building is worth glancing up to see. Courtesy of Jeannine Levesque

A placid view of South Main Street around 1907 shows the clipper shop in left background. The intersection of Lake Street and Main Street is at right center. The lack of traffic is a striking feature of this photo which appears to have been taken on a fine summer day.
Courtesy of Paul Newman, from his postcard collection

The Frank Anderson mansion at 90 Concord Street, built in 1905, was by far the most ostentatious and elaborate house of all the great Concord Street houses. It even had its own theater and the dining room was oval-shaped. The grounds and gardens were magnificent. Anderson was a prominent shoe manufacturer. The house is now owned by Mt. St. Mary Seminary, a private school for girls.
Courtesy of Frank Mooney

Luther Abbot Roby owned a large farm on Spitbrook Road that his grandchildren, the Swart children, loved to visit. Roby was a remarkable man whose very long life was devoted to several interests. In his youth he ran canal boats on the Merrimack. In later years he built up a lumber business that specialized in ships' timbers. In this snapshot we see him in spry old age enjoying the role of gentleman farmer.
Courtesy of Margaret Beasom Swart

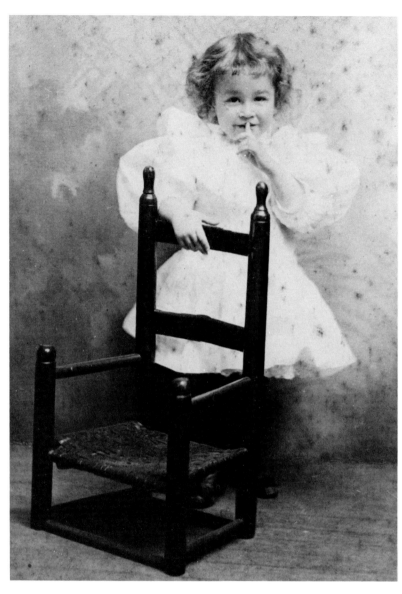

In the Edwardian age it was not at all unusual for boy babies to be dressed in girls' clothes, especially if they were having their pictures taken. This toddler with the coy look was, believe it or not, Roby Swart, late treasurer of the Telegraph Publishing Company.
Courtesy of Margaret Beasom Swart

In 1905 smart-looking horse-and-buggy combinations were still a favored way to get around town. This snapshot was taken in the driveway of the Swart home at 92 Concord Street. In 1987 this house was used as a "Decorators' Showcase" to raise money for the Nashua Symphony.
Courtesy of Margaret Beasom Swart

121

This house at 94 Concord Street was the residence of Gen. and Mrs. Elbert Wheeler. Wheeler was a West Point graduate and his title of ''General'' came from his leadership in the New Hampshire National Guard which he helped to develop. His wife was a daughter of Luther A. Roby. Another Roby daughter married William D. Swart. The Wheelers and the Swarts lived next door to each other. Wheeler was a strong advocate of women's suffrage and played an active role in organizations promoting this movement.
Courtesy of Margaret Beasom Swart

The carriage houses of the Concord Street houses were almost as elaborate as the homes. This is the carriage house of the Wheeler residence. The bird bath has the date 1903 inscribed on it.
Courtesy of Margaret Beasom Swart

General and Mrs. Wheeler are seen here in an automobile of obviously very early vintage. The city directories at the time actually listed owners and the makes of the vehicles they drove. The residents of the big Concord Street houses were, of course, among those who quickly converted to the use of "horseless carriages." According to the directory of 1906, General Wheeler owned a 3.5 horsepower Columbia.
Courtesy of Margaret Beasom Swart

The Beasom family moved to a house built for them at 77 Concord Street in 1913. This is Mrs. William H. Beasom in front of this home. She was a lady noted for her involvement in charitable works and church affairs.
Courtesy of Margaret Beasom Swart, her daughter

Margaret Beasom Swart is seen here as a teenager sitting on the front steps of her parents' home.
Courtesy of Margaret Beasom Swart

Members of some of the Concord Street families enjoyed Thanksgiving together in 1914. From left to right: Clara Wheeler, Elbert Wheeler, Lizzie Swart, Betty Swart McQueston, Dr. Sam Dearborn, William Dummond Swart, Mrs. Sam Dearborn, and William Roby Swart.
Courtesy of Margaret Beasom Swart

William Dummond Swart, the owner of the house at 92 Concord Street, enjoyed bicycle riding. He was the publisher of the Nashua Telegraph and was involved in other business enterprises. His son, William Roby Swart, married Margaret Beasom in 1927, uniting two of the prominent Concord Street families. Courtesy of Margaret Beasom Swart

By the twenties the young people in the Concord Street families were driving this type of car. These wealthy and prominent citizens led pleasant lives in which great emphasis was placed on strong family ties and social responsibility. Courtesy of Margaret Beasom Swart whose photograph albums present a fascinating picture of the conservative and solid life style of the era of the early part of this century

The donor of this photograph was able to date it when he gave it to the library—September 10, 1905, when the crew of Marshall's Livery Stable on Mellin Court off Canal Street lined up to have their picture taken. Livery stables provided much the same service that car rental firms do today.
NPL file photograph

Architecturally the Post Office that stood on Court Street from 1906 until 1970 (used as a post office until 1963) was a magnificent edifice. Parking space for both the public and the postal staff, however, was totally inadequate for modern needs. The courtyard of the Nashua Public Library was laid out on its site.
Courtesy of Nancy Atherton Buell

126

The City Farm on Taylor Road was Nashua's poorhouse until 1908 when it was closed as an outdated institution. Prisoners who had been convicted of minor offenses were also kept there. A husband and wife team managed the farm and house and inmates did the chores; able-bodied males worked on the town roads. Courtesy of Paul Newman, from his postcard collection

This is a view of the same house and barn in the early twenties after the property had been the Nashua Country Club for several years. The Nashua Development Corporation bought the farm and its 160 acres of pastureland, renovated the house, and laid out an eighteen-hole golf course. In August 1916, it was officially opened. Courtesy of Paul Newman, from his postcard collection

Harbor Pond was part of the Salmon Brook system. This photo was taken around 1910 when it was a popular spot for swimming in the summer and ice skating in the winter. Eventually it became polluted and complaints about unhealthy conditions led to the city starting to fill it in the late forties. By 1962 Simoneau Plaza and its parking lot completely covered the site. The mall experienced problems with the ground settling, causing sloping floors in stores. Courtesy of Paul Newman, from his postcard collection

*The accompanying map section will clarify
the location of these falls. There are
persons still living who remember as
youngsters using this bridge as a shortcut
to the Marshall Street area. Salmon Brook
is now largely underground on the east
side of Main Street. At one time it emptied
with a splash from these falls on the
southern side of Harbor Pond, then continued on its way to the Merrimack
through an outlet that was also on the
southern side. An idyllic scene from the
Nashua of long ago!*
*Courtesy of Paul Newman,
from his postcard collection;
map portion from 1883 Nashua map,
Puritan Press, 1982*

This is a lucky action shot taken around 1910. The driver of the three-in-hand team was a well-known fireman who had great skill in managing horses. He had apparently borrowed an old stagecoach for this demonstration. There are three differ-ent forms of transportation in one picture: the coach, the trolley, and the automobile. The building in the background was the old Telegraph Block.
Courtesy of Janet Atherton Snow

The best guess for the date of this unique shot is 1910. Hammar Hardware had not as yet moved into the ground floor of the Laton Building where it would do business until the seventies. At the time of the photo the space was occupied by the Nashua Harness Company. The Hunt Library was starting to be covered with its first growth of ivy. An interesting feature of the snappy-looking roadster is the steering wheel on the right side—perhaps, in fact undoubtedly, a British import. The street cleaner has his wheelbarrow close at hand as he sweeps the cobblestones.

Courtesy of Margaret Beasom Swart

Frank Flynn is given as the name of this man who cleaned the streets of Nashua for many years. Although the picture is rather dim, this is a valuable souvenir of a public employee who performed such a necessary task day after day. It could not have been an easy or pleasant job, especially when there were several hundred horses on the streets of the city.
NPL file photograph

The original St. Joseph's Hospital was dedicated in 1908. It was an achievement of the legendary Father Millette of St. Louis de Gonzague Church. The new St.

Joseph's Hospital was built in 1967 on the same Kinsley Street site.
Courtesy of Alfred Lawrence

This building at the corner of Court and Park streets was the John G. Foster Post, Grand Army of the Republic (Post No. 7). Members of the post made careful arrangements for the time when their organization would no longer exist. The last Civil War veteran in Nashua died in 1937. In 1952 the local post of the Disabled American Veterans bought the building and moved it to Cross Street.
Courtesy of Nancy Atherton Buell

Believe it or not, this was Amherst Street in the halcyon days before commercial strip development. The photo shows a section called the "Willows" because of the thick growth of over-arching trees. Just beyond to the right was the Kessler Farm. It was so little traveled that it was a favorite route for bicyclists.
NPL file photograph

This is a view looking south on Amherst Street at about the same time. If the fence on the lefthand side looks vaguely familiar, it is because it is still there. It encloses the Roby Cemetery which was laid out in 1813. All of the gravestones in this small cemetery are dated in the nineteenth century. A full list of the persons buried there appears in Parker's History of Nashua.
NPL file photograph

In March 1912, President William Howard Taft came to Nashua to lay the cornerstone of the YMCA Building on Temple Street. He is the rotund figure beside the block and tackle underneath the flag. Although one or two security guards seem to be watching the crowd, a president would not be allowed this close to his audience today.
A postcard from the NPL file

The second photograph of the Taft visit to Nashua shows him leaving his car. Here, too, security seems casual by present day standards. The presidential visit was a gala event, attended by much excitement. NPL file photograph

This advertising postcard shows a beauty shop around 1915. Miss Mary Taunt was an enterprising woman who built a career as a chiropodist and a cosmetician. She was a good example of the many women who, even in the earlier part of this century, earned their own living. The rattan furniture seen in the shop was very popular during this period. The hair dryer had not, of course, yet been invented. Courtesy of Paul Newman, from his postcard collection

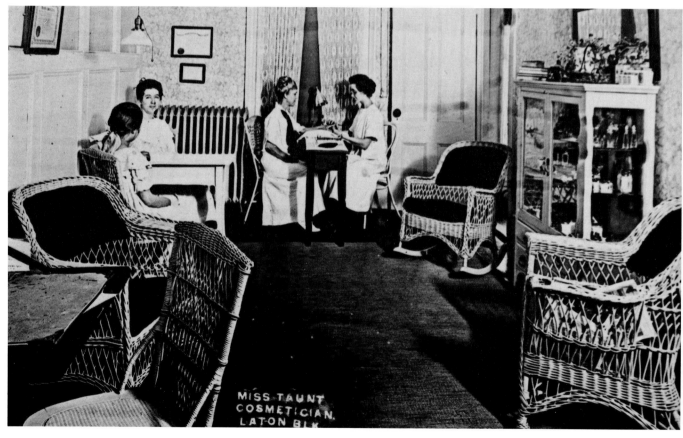

MISS TAUNT
COSMETICIAN.
LATON BLK

During the bitter 1915 strike the state militia was sent down to Nashua to assist in the situation. They are seen here massed in front of the administration building.
Courtesy of Frank Mooney

Noon Hour, Nashua Manufacturing Co.,
Nashua, N. H.

This very elaborate and detailed rendering of the Nashua Manufacturing Company mills as they looked around 1915 hung for many years in the office of the Nashua-New Hampshire Foundation. It is about six feet long.
Courtesy of the present owners,
Mr. and Mrs. Richard West;
photograph by Brian Lawrence

This was Factory Street on a sunny spring day around 1917. During their lunch period many of the mill workers are enjoying the fresh air. The houses on the far left were originally boarding houses for the "Yankee Mill Girls."
Courtesy of Paul Newman,
from his postcard collection

135

"The parade is over—let's go home to dinner!" This famous photo has invariably brought the reaction from viewers that "It looks like a Keystone Kops movie scene." Nobody seems to be concerned about traffic lights or "Walk" and "Don't Walk" signs. Antique car buffs might like to try dating it from the variety of vehicles. The best guess is probably 1919.
NPL file photograph

The class of 1916, Nashua High School, poses for a group picture outside the High School on Temple Street. Blanche Nutting Bickford, second from the right in the second row, is one of the few members of this class still alive. She was the daughter of William Nutting, the founder of Nutting's Music Store.
Courtesy of Blanche Nutting Bickford

136

The Chase Building was erected on the site formerly occupied by the Beasom House. At the time it was considered a major step in transforming this part of Main Street into a modern business district. The Beasom property was bought in March 1916, by the Amoskeag Real Estate Company of Manchester. The building was named in honor of the president of this company, E. M. Chase. Although original plans called for a four-story building, the three-story structure probably resulted in better proportions. A new theater called the Tremont occupied part of the building. In the late twenties this theater would be moved across the street to the Merchants Exchange; the State Theater moved into the space in the Chase Building. Historic preservationists could point to what has happened to this building over the years as an object lesson on the need to maintain the integrity of architecture.
Courtesy of Alfred Lawrence

A closeup of the second-story arch as it appears today shows how well the Chase Building has weathered time.
Courtesy of Jeannine Levesque who has conducted historic walking tours called "A Step Above Main Street"

The "clipper shop" on Main Street across the street from IPBMC (shown in next photograph) was the plant of the American Shearing Company which was an important industry from 1865 until 1950. Sheep shearers were invented by J. K. Priest and Roswell T. Smith. They also made barber clippers and similar types of tools. This plant was torn down in 1972 when Simoneau Plaza was expanded.
Courtesy of Alfred Lawrence

The International Paper Box Machinery Company was a highly successful enterprise founded in 1903 by Elie W. Labombarde at the site of the old Vale Mills. The company is still in business but is now located on Northeastern Boulevard. The illustration is from their fiftieth anniversary booklet.

Holbrook Marshall was a wholesale grocery company that operated in this building on East Hollis Street from 1905 to 1943. The postcard was an advertising card on which the sender mentioned that it was one of three such plants that the company had. When the Matthew Thornton Health Plan made plans to establish an east side branch, they bought the old building and did a remarkable job of transforming it into a modern medical center. It is an excellent example of a new use for an old facility.
Courtesy of Paul Newman, from his postcard collection

This was how the Masonic Temple looked on Armistice Day in 1918, eloquently expressing the universal joy that World War I was over. The Colonial Theater entrance can be seen on the other side of the building. The touring car and the sedan parked further down the street were typical of the vehicles being driven by Nashuans at this period.
Courtesy of Robert Pinsonneault

In February and March of 1920 the city
was hit by several bad storms, one on top of
another. Mayor Henri Burque in despera-
tion organized citizen shoveling teams to
assist in clearing the streets of accumulated
snow. One newspaper headline read
"Shovelites at South End," another
"Shoveling Bee Goes Merrily On." It was
a community crisis that brought everyone
together in a cooperative effort. Here is
what Court Street looked like after the last
snowstorm in March of that winter.
Courtesy of Paul Newman,
from his postcard collection

The main station of the Pennichuck Water
Works is shown here in the twenties. In
1978 the institution received an award
and was designated a Civil Engineering
Historical Site.
Courtesy of Nancy Atherton Buell

The Universalist Church and vicinity in the early twenties is shown in this snapshot. At left are the house and office of Dr. Evan Hammond which in the late thirties were torn down to provide a site for the Professional Building (former home of Sears Roebuck). The church was used for various commercial purposes after the Universalists merged with the Unitarians in 1957. It has now been remodelled and named City Plaza.
Courtesy of Nancy Atherton Buell

On March 14, 1922, Nashua firefighters were faced with one of the worst fires in their history. The Telegraph Block, erected in 1871 at Main and Temple streets, blazed furiously for hours. The building was owned by the Indian Head Bank. The newspaper that built it had moved out in 1909.
Courtesy of Paul Newman, from his postcard collection

Only the ground floor of the Telegraph Block was undamaged enough to permit the bank to move its operations back into it for a few months. Until construction of the new bank building began, this was how the Main and Temple street corner looked.
Courtesy of Frank Mooney

The Indian Head Bank building was erected on the Temple Street corner in 1924. A detail from its pediment is shown in a camera shot taken by Jeannine Levesque.

142

These two snapshots, taken by an amateur photographer who did not hold the camera quite straight, show almost the entire length of the Merchants Exchange as it looked in the 1920s. Some of the ornamentation uncovered during the recent restoration can be seen around the doorway to the left of the Ideal Lunch. The marquee was not advertising a movie; the signs read "J. C. Trombloom—Boys' Wear—Mens' Wear." Courtesy of Nancy Atherton Buell who found a book with many Nashua snapshots taken by students among her grandmother's belongings.

On February 16, 1930, a fire caused
$90,000 worth of damage to the Merchants
Exchange at its northern end. This end
was rebuilt after the fire. The old building
is indeed a "survivor." On January 6,
1989, the restoration project, complete
with the exciting new Martha's Exchange
restaurant and function rooms, was given
the Mayor's Blue Ribbon Award for excel-
lence in preservation of an historic building. The citation stated that the project
served as a superior model for others and
made a major contribution to the revitali-
zation of the city's downtown area.
Courtesy of Alfred Lawrence

In the 1920s Jeannotte's Furniture Store
was located in the Phillips Block. The
building was burned down in 1961.
Courtesy of Nancy Atherton Buell

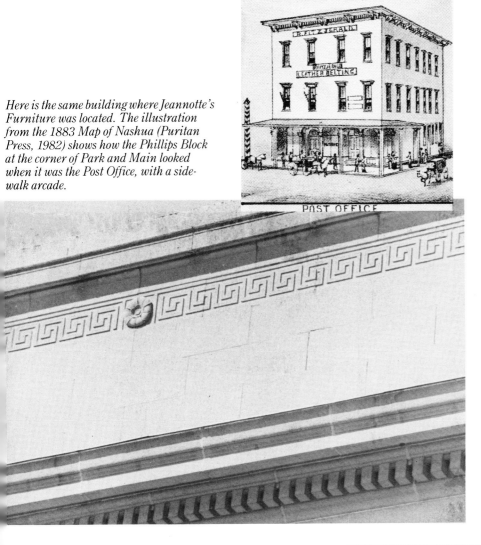

POST OFFICE

Here is the same building where Jeannotte's Furniture was located. The illustration from the 1883 Map of Nashua (Puritan Press, 1982) shows how the Phillips Block at the corner of Park and Main looked when it was the Post Office, with a sidewalk arcade.

This is a detail of the tasteful and restrained ornamentation on the top of the side facade of the Bank of New Hampshire. The building, when erected in 1924, was the home of the Second National Bank. In this one year there was a big leap in modernization of downtown.
Courtesy of Jeannine Levesque

These businesses were located in the Bowers Block at 69 Main Street. The "Paris" catered to both men and women shopping for fashionable clothing. Downstairs, Slawsby's Cash Market was running a special on corned beef. If this block seems quite crowded with buildings, compared with how it looks today, the answer is that Water Street was probably somewhat narrower and the Bicentennial Park was not in existence at the time; there were buildings all the way to the bridge.
Courtesy of Nancy Atherton Buell

*A view of Main Street in the mid-twenties
is a mixture of the new (the bank building
on the corner of West Pearl), the old (the
Parkinson Building), and the future (the
vacant lot where the Public Service
Building would soon rise).
Courtesy of Alfred Lawrence*

C. H. Avery Company celebrates its centennial at the same time as the Nashua Trust Company—1989. The store that has sold high quality furniture to Nashua households for one hundred years on Factory Street suffered a disastrous fire in 1925. Phoenix-like, it rose from its ashes and continued in business.
NPL file photograph

On December 11, 1924, Main Street Bridge burned down, the debris crashing into the river.
Courtesy of Paul Newman, from his postcard collection

As shown in the bottom picture, some residents took to rowboats to get from one side of town to the other. A temporary wooden replacement was soon in place but it was not until June 1927 that the permanent bridge was finally open to traffic. This new bridge was called the widest bridge for its length in the world.
Courtesy of Paul Newman, from his postcard collection

City Hall casts its shadow from across the
street in three snapshots which, taken
together, will give some idea of the former
appearance of the west side of Main Street.
First is the Beasom Block, a building that
throughout its history of about 120 years
seemed jinxed by fire. Yet many gala social
events were held in its top floor function
rooms. After the last Beasom Block was
destroyed in 1961, the block that replaced
it was given a different name—Patriot's
Block.

These are the Ridgway Building, the
Goddard Building, and the Second
National Bank Building.

The Howard Building, later known as the Montcalm Building, was often referred to as the Crescent Building because of its curved facade. This block was put up during the 1880s by Joseph W. Howard and his father, Ezra P. Howard. Joseph Howard was a furniture manufacturer and retailer who was part of the Nashua business world for many years. The Howards must have been very imaginative people to have conceived the idea, already used in Bath, England, of a crescent-shaped building as the best way to deal with a site that jutted out at a narrower part of the street. This unique building was demolished in the widening of Main Street.
All snapshots courtesy of Nancy Atherton Buell

The small boys trying to decide what to spend their pennies on at Duhamel's Candy Store may bring back memories of childhood days. The store was on West *Hollis Street for many years. The building is still standing.*
Courtesy of Alfred Lawrence

Main Street is decked in bunting for the celebration of the city's seventy-fifth anniversary in 1928. The banner hung overhead reads "Why not have a big time?" The curve of the Montcalm Building shows up especially well here. NPL file photograph

New England Tel and Tel employees contributed a float to the "big time" celebration.
Courtesy of Patty Ledoux

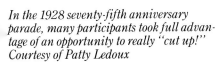

In the 1928 seventy-fifth anniversary parade, many participants took full advantage of an opportunity to really "cut up!"
Courtesy of Patty Ledoux

Two beautiful horses pull a circus wagon full of merrymakers, one enthusiastically beating a drum, in the 1928 parade.
Courtesy of Patty Ledoux

GREEK COMMUNITY PARTICIPATION IN 75TH ANNIVERSARY CELEBRATION OF THE CITY OF NASHUA — 1928.

Courtesy of Alfred Lawrence

This photo of the Nashua Telegraph Building was probably taken soon after it was ready for occupancy in 1928. The billboard on the roof to the left advertised "Moxie," a popular soft drink of that period. Today the building has been renovated for use as office space. It no longer reverberates with the thunder of the printing presses—the newspaper moved to larger quarters in Hudson several years ago.
NPL file photograph

The Proctor Cemetery for Animals was started on available land on the Ferry Hill Road in the 1920s. The cemetery which has grown greatly since this early picture was taken is administered by the Nashua Humane Society. A new modern building was finally erected for this society, which does such important work in caring for homeless animals, in 1978.
NPL file photograph

152

Here is a rare photo of the Field's Grove swimming area, probably taken in the twenties. This recreational spot, where hundreds of Nashua children took Red Cross swimming lessons, was named for a landholder who generously allowed access to it through his property. Eventually pollution of the Salmon Brook, of which it was a part, forced the city to close the area. The happy news at the present time is that the area is to be reopened in the future as a badly needed South End park.
NPL file photograph

This large photograph (the original is over three feet long) shows the extent of the devastation caused by the big fire of May 4, 1930. Four hundred families lost their homes and several industrial concerns were burned out. About a quarter of the city was destroyed. Relief efforts were started immediately to assist the people who had lost everything they owned. It was a tragic time for Nashua but also a proud time because of the efficiency with which rebuilding was undertaken. The photograph was taken near Bowers Street by a Haverhill photographer, Charles Palmer.
Courtesy of Patty Ledoux

The chapel-school of Infant Jesus Church looks like a bombed-out European cathedral in this photo taken after the big fire. The structure was rebuilt in less than a year. Because of the depression the parish had to abandon its plans to build a separate church. The present Infant Jesus church was erected in 1955. During the fire a curate heroically led 700 children to safety from the third floor of the chapel-school.
Courtesy of Alfred Lawrence

153

A remarkable fact about the great fire of 1930 is that someone with a camera actually snapped a picture of the place where the fire started. It began underneath this trestle that bridged the river behind the Jackson Mills. A strong wind on that Sunday afternoon in May carried embers toward the Crown Hill area. The flames spread so fast from one house to another that they defeated the best efforts of fire companies from many miles around. W. F. Sullivan, chief of the Nashua Fire Department at the time, wrote a dramatic description of the crisis in the Journal of the New England Water Association. *NPL file photograph*

It is April 19, 1931, and the old City Station, built in 1848, has just been completely gutted by fire. The Franklin Opera House on the second floor was host to many troupes of entertainers who played to audiences there. The admission price for the movies it showed was regularly advertised as five cents. On the same weekend, the famous Nashua Theater on Elm Street was also the victim of fire. NPL file photograph

154

In June 1933, Nashua High School class of 1883 held their fiftieth reunion in Dunstable, Massachusetts. The group photograph of members of the class and guests is captioned as follows. First row, left to right, are Mrs. Sanderson, Lizzie Case Sulham, Miss Eagan, Miss Gorman, Mr. Sanderson, Mr. Washburn, Miss Preston, Miss McClure, Margie Gregg Hussey, and Miss Farley. Second row, left to right, are Maggie Sullivan Cote, Mrs. Sullivan (widow of Patrick Sullivan), Miss Crowley (sister of James B. Crowley), Miss Reed, Mrs. Shea (widow of Dr. Augustus Shea), Mrs. Kendrick (widow of Arthur Kendrick), Fanny Lane Colburn, Grace Gage Hubbard, Miss Harlow, and Miss Hubbard (daughter of Mrs. Hubbard).
NPL file photograph

155

A special part of the Pennichuck woods was dedicated as the Frank G. Blanchard Reservation on September 28, 1933. Here is a group of prominent citizens who were interested in seeing that these woodlands should be kept for sports and recreation. At the far left, the gentleman holding the fishing pole is Mayor William Sullivan. On his left is Philip Morris and next is William H. Beasom who was a noted out-door sportsman. The two men in the center of the group are Thomas Leonard and T. H. Barnard. The identities of the three men at right are not known.
NPL file photograph

This building was torn down to provide the site for the new City Hall. Workmen engaged in the demolition discovered evidence that it was built in 1851. For many years a private residence, it became the headquarters of the Holy Name Society of St. Patrick's Church in 1925.
NPL file photograph

The dress shop tucked into a corner of the house is a good example of what happened to some of the fine old residences on Main Street. They would be taken over for business use before finally undergoing

demolition so that a large, modern block could be built on the site. Diners, of course, have become outmoded as eateries. Another very popular diner, located on the east side of Main Street, was the "Yankee Flyer."

Many older people recall the good meals, often including home-baked pastries, that they ate there.
NPL file photograph

Here the old City Hall seems to be posing for a formal portrait in the last days of its existence. Although it was a well-proportioned building, its fine exterior reflecting the ability of its architect, Samuel Shepherd, it had deteriorated badly.
NPL file photograph

Almost one hundred years of history passed into memory as the old City Hall was taken down in 1939/40. Along with it the Municipal Records Building was also demolished. When the cornerstone of the City Hall was finally located and opened in April 1940, the names of the building committee were found inscribed on a tablet. The beautiful wrought iron railings are now part of the staircase at the Speare Building of the Historical Society; in this way something that belonged to the old building has been preserved.
NPL file photograph

Frank Ingalls was on hand with his camera when officials gathered in the narrow alley beside the Nelson Building to witness the opening of the cornerstone of the old City Hall on April 24, 1940. In the foreground, left to right, are Fred Dobens, editor of the Nashua Telegraph*; Annie L. Goodrich of the Historical Society; Irenee D. Ravenelle, city clerk; and Mayor Eugene H. Lemay.*
NPL file photograph

This is how Holman Stadium looked when it had just been built. The stadium itself was a memorial gift from Frank Holman in honor of his parents; the money being left in his will. The federal government provided WPA funds to grade the field.

The Knights of Columbus donated the additional steel bleachers, making the total capacity of the stadium four thousand. With recent additions it seats twice that number. A crowd as large as fifteen thousand, many bringing their own folding

chairs, has filled bleachers and the field for community events such as the annual Fourth of July concert and fireworks. Photograph taken by Ingalls in July 1937; NPL file

On August 25, 1931, Mayor William F. Sullivan and other city officials dedicated a huge gate beside the highway at the state line. It symbolized Nashua's pride in being the "Gate City."
NPL file photograph

There seems to have been a little accident at Al's Variety Store on Harbor Avenue. The incident occurred back in 1939. The young spectators are obviously awed that a truck could crash right into the store.
Courtesy of Patty Ledoux

The Kernwood Hotel stood on the west side of upper Main Street from 1930 until it ·burned down in 1965. It was a hotel for the budget-minded traveler, offering thirty-five rooms, two dining rooms, and the "Brick Oven" coffee shop.
Courtesy of Paul Newman,
from his postcard collection

The Public Service Building went up in 1930, another major step in creating a modern business district. The exterior decorations are beautiful. Shown here is a closeup of one of the windows.
Courtesy of Jeannine Levesque

An inspiring success story in Nashua business history is that of the LaRose family and their Modern Restaurant. Although as of the time this was written the famous restaurant had closed its doors, it served the public for over fifty years. In this photograph, taken in 1935, are four of the people who worked at the Modern in its early days. A happy postscript to this caption is that, as this book goes to press, the Modern has reopened.
Courtesy of Alfred Lawrence

Scouting has always been an important part of youth activity in Nashua. This cheerful-looking group was Troop 20 of the Boy Scouts of America, Daniel Webster Council. The photograph was taken in 1947.
Courtesy of Alfred Lawrence

The Board of Public Works around 1940
is shown here in a formal portrait. Back
row, left to right, are Theodore Hudon,
Claude Raby, John Diggins, and Joseph
Bouchard. Front row, left to right, are
Fred L. Clark, city engineer; Mayor

Eugene Lemay; and William Tolles,
superintendent of streets.
Courtesy of M. Theresa Hamel, Mr.
Hudon's daughter, who donated the
photograph to the library

The Chamber of Commerce sponsored industrial fairs as far back as 1923. In this one held during the forties the exhibits were quite elaborate and sophisticated. The Nashua Mike and Key Club, shown demonstrating its work, was a very active organization, as at that time many people were interested in amateur radio.
Courtesy of Alfred Lawrence

The Nashua Manufacturing Company's exhibit featured a "Jacquard loom making name stripe for Dwight Anchor Sheets."
Courtesy of Alfred Lawrence

Restaurant

Main Lobby

Laton Hotel

Nashua,
N. H.

*The original postcard from which this copy was made is in very vivid colors. The mansard top of the hotel is painted pale green, the rest of the building is red, the seats in the restaurant are blue, and the upholstery and carpeting in the lobby are red. The photo was probably taken in the last part of the period (1912-1948) when the Pentland family ran the Laton House. It is described as "one of Southern New Hampshire's finer hotels." After this period it suffered from competition with motels and began to deteriorate. It is still a picturesque building that has played an important part in Nashua's history.
Courtesy of Paul Newman,
from his postcard collection*

*Automobile experts can probably date this picture quite closely by studying the cars parked in front of the Green Ridge Turkey Farm. This is one of Nashua's most durable restaurants, still popular even though there are no longer pens where the turkeys were raised in its back yard.
Courtesy of Janet Atherton Snow*

At Christmas 1941, the directors of the
Nashua Trust Company were photo-
graphed for the bank's greeting card. Front
row, left to right, are Richard Cook;
Timothy F. Rock, M.D.; Raymond H.
Marcotte, M.D.; and Charles H. Austin.
Second row, left to right, are Thomas J.
Dowd, Alfred C. Lacaillade, Roscoe M.
Woodward, Walter F. Norton, Francis P.
Murphy, George E. Harris, Joseph L.
Clough, and Henri T. Ledoux.
NPL file

On May 28, 1945, a group of librarians
representing the southern part of the state
in the New Hampshire Library Association posed for this group photo before a
meeting in Nashua. The gentleman at the
right in the third row is Judge John R.
Spring who was secretary of the Nashua
Library Board of Trustees. Other Nashua
people are Marion Manning, Children's
Librarian at NPL until 1968, first row at
left; Etta Lovejoy, fourth from left in first
row; Clara E. Smith, NPL librarian until
1952, second from right in first row;
Christine Rockwood, at left in second row;

Dorothy Harris, at left in back row; and
Rachel Sanborn, fourth from left in back
row.

Photograph from a Nashua Public Library
publicity scrapbook

166

This was the scene at Crowley School on "Library Day" in 1946. Perhaps some of the children, now middle-aged people, will recognize themselves in the photo. The James B. Crowley School on Lake Street was an elementary school for over sixty years. After the school department made the decision to close the school, it became the headquarters of the Adult Learning Center.

Photo from a Nashua Public Library publicity scrapbook

The Coffey Post Band, American Legion, was photographed during an engagement at the State House in Concord on an undetermined date. The band played on many occasions and was a familiar part of all parades. It has now merged with the Hudson American Legion band.
NPL file photograph

The Order of Ahepa sponsored a youth band known as the John F. Davis Drum and Bugle Corps that won several trophies. The exact date of this photograph is unknown, but this is certainly a fine-looking group of boys.
Courtesy of Alfred Lawrence

A patriotic parade, probably on a Memorial Day after World War II, comes down Library Hill. It is an interesting note that tanks were displayed for the occasion. Photograph by Fotomart; courtesy of Patty Ledoux

It was a very proud and happy day, May 18, 1944, when the Nashua cotton mills were honored with an "E" award for their production in connection with the war effort. Many photographs were taken to record the occasion. Here a group of employees heads down to the bleachers that were erected in front of the mills at NMC. Courtesy of Patty Ledoux

The mill building and grounds appear here at their immaculate best, as the company prepares to receive its "E" award. In four years time there would be no more Nashua Manufacturing Company. Today the buildings are being renovated into housing units. The development has been named Clocktower Place. Courtesy of Patty Ledoux

*Here is another picture taken on "E" Day
in 1944. The Jackson Mills on Canal
Street, producers of the famous Indian
Head cloth, participated in the awards. As
the sign indicates, the two mills were
under the same management.
Courtesy of Patty Ledoux*

It is reassuring to see the Nashua Trust clock in place even in this photo taken in an earlier part of the century. Before its removal to the Masonic Temple in 1900 the bank's offices were in the McQuesten Building. In a later remodeling the corner with the post was closed in. The traffic light on the post makes dating this picture problematic. The need for a traffic light system was discussed by the aldermen during the twenties but it took some time before the idea was put into effect. The light was probably operated manually by a policeman.
Courtesy of Alfred Lawrence

William H. Beasom was the son of William D. Beasom who built the first Beasom Block. He became mayor of Nashua in 1890 when he was only twenty-nine years old. He had a long and distinguished career as an industrialist and was involved in many Nashua happenings. Born in 1861, he lived to witness World War II. Margaret Beasom Swart, the widow of William Roby Swart of the Telegraph, was his youngest daughter. She is still an active member of the Nashua community, with a special interest in the Nashua Center for the Arts. NPL file photograph

Mrs. Nellie F. Woodward, a doctor's wife, lived from 1854 to 1930. She is remembered as a glowing example of the many Nashua women who served both community and state through club activities. She was at one time president of the New Hampshire Federation of Women's Clubs. Deeply concerned about the need for conservation of forests and other natural resources, she worked very hard in the final days of her life to save Franconia Notch and the Old Man of the Mountains. NPL file photograph

Artist's Concept of Gateway Center

*This artist's concept of the projected
Gateway Center in downtown Nashua
shows how a twelve-story building will
change the profile of this business district.
Courtesy of the Downtown Development
Corporation*

5

ANNALS OF MODERN NASHUA: 1951-1988

Many older residents speak wistfully of the days "when we used to be like a small town where everyone knew everyone else." Out of the explosive boom of these last four decades a whole new city seems to have evolved. Huge apartment complexes have sprouted on the horizons, country roads have become commercial strips, traffic has become "as bad as Boston." Although many regret the loss of the old type of cohesiveness, many others have found the rapid changes exciting.

Thousands of newcomers have brought much more than the furniture in the moving vans with them. They have also brought new ideas, sophisticated tastes, urban lifestyles. Nashua is no longer an average New England town. As if to dramatize this point, a national magazine in 1987 ranked the city "Number One" on a list of the most desirable communities in the country in which to live. Proving how unreliable such heady honors can be, in 1988 this same magazine ranked the city in sixth place. To emphasize still further the amazing growth, the Office of State Planning projects that in twenty years Nashua will outstrip Manchester in size.

How important is local history to these recent new residents and how important will it be to those yet to come? Will they be able to see beneath the burgeoning profile of the city's new look the people and events that have shaped its identity for three hundred years? One can only hope that enough visible clues of the past have been preserved to convey some immediate sense of what Nashua is all about. Herein lies the value of historic preservation, of making wise decisions about the symbols of that past that should be protected and proudly displayed.

Presented here are some happenings selected from the annals of the years 1951 through 1988.

1951: Nashua's Main Street was declared the most traveled highway in the state. Claude Nichols served the second year of Hugh Gregg's term as mayor; Gregg had been recalled to military service. In the November election Lester Burnham was elected mayor. Doehla Greeting Cards moved to Nashua from Fitchburg.

1952: Sanders Associates was formed, buying the old Jackson Mills facility on Canal Street. This company, now owned by Lockheed, has been a phenomenally successful electronics manufacturer. Planning was started for a bypass highway. The cornerstone was laid for St. Christopher's Church on Manchester Street.

1953: The big event was the giant centennial celebration which included a parade that featured the Ferko string band of Philadelphia. The festivities brought the whole city together as one big family expressing pride in one hundred years of progress. There was a strong sense of awareness of the historical background that had forged the city. Hugh Gregg became governor of New Hampshire. Alvin A. Lucier, ex-mayor and political satirist, died. "Birdie" Tebbetts, a hometown boy who made good in baseball, was named manager of the Cincinnati Reds.

1954: The Frederick E. Everett Highway was opened. Two new elementary schools were Charlotte Avenue and Fairgrounds. The Friendship Club, a long-needed gathering place for handicapped people, became a reality on Orchard Heights. Hurricane Carol did considerable damage, most notably to the Pilgrim Church. Nashua High School won state football title for third straight year. Bad train crash at Union Station.

1955: Centennial Pool near Holman Stadium opened. Burnham won third term as mayor. Nashua High won state title for fourth year. Indian Head Bank bought Pilgrim Church site. Industrial growth and a record number of permits for new houses was registered.

1956: Still another new elementary school was opened—Ledge Street, as the school population reached an all-time high of over seventy-three hundred. Planning started for Main Street widening project. The Board of Education banned blue jeans and Elvis Presley haircuts!

1957: Nashua considered to be fastest growing city in state. Armory on Canal Street burned down. The recently merged Unitarian-Universalist Church bought the site for expansion of its facilities. The new Pilgrim Church on Watson Street was dedicated.

1958: Mario Vagge became mayor. Edmund M. Keefe named superintendent of schools. Memorial Hospital expansion built. Sensational story of year was the Carol Foster counterspy revelation.

1959: Widening of Main Street at end near bridge completed. Nashua bypass opened as four-lane highway. Temple Beth Abraham dedicated new temple on Raymond Street. Three million dollar fire at 82 Main Street. Mabel Chandler left her home to the city as a branch library. Mayor Vagge was reelected. Martineau and Nelson murder trial.

1960: Nashua's population forty thousand. John F. Kennedy opened his campaign for the presidency in front of Nashua's City Hall—commemorated by his bust erected there after the assassination. The Chandler Memorial Library at 257 Main Street was opened. New State Armory completed.

1961: The Beasom Block burned down again! Ground broken for new FAA control tower. New bridge over Merrimack needed but controversy with town of Hudson had begun. Third term for Mayor Vagge.

1962: Low-rent housing project, Vagge Village, ready for tenants. Simoneau Plaza, Nashua's first shopping mall, opened—built on filled Harbor Pond. Water Street ramp completed. Hearing conducted on charges of racial discrimination in Myrtle Street housing. School officials pass ruling against girls wearing wigs.

1963: First housing code passed by aldermen. New Post Office on Spring Street placed in operation; there were immediate complaints about the parking space being "the size of a postage stamp." Ten thousand people toured the new FAA Center. Mayor Vagge was elected for a fourth term. High Street development area included a huge supermarket built by 20th Century Markets. The city bought a rubbish burner for the West Hollis Street dump. Memorial Hospital completed its new wing. Weatherwise this was a year of drought.

1964: Another summer of drought—Pennichuck restricted the use of water. Bishop Guertin High School for boys opened. Continued dispute over replacement for Taylor Falls Bridge. South End liquor store was built. The YMCA/YWCA building on Prospect Street was completed.

1965: The Sullivan Era began when Dennis J. Sullivan was elected mayor in November. The next eleven years would be marked by extreme conservatism at City Hall. Sullivan's reelections by overwhelming majorities possibly reflected the culture shock felt by long-established residents in the face of the rapid growth, combined with indifference by new residents to local politics. New England Aeronautical Institute was started at Boire Field; this has now become a full four-year college, Daniel Webster College. Mt. St. Mary School for girls began classes in the former Anderson house on Concord Street. One majestic old landmark that suffered demolition (and should have been preserved) was Union Station. Delay over new bridge continued.

1966: Bond issue resolution for construction of interceptors passed as a pollution control measure. Richard Chaput, local paralytic, flew to midwest to be honored as one of the "Young Men of the Year" by Jaycees. Low-rent housing complex on Ledge Street was turned over to the city.

Spring Street School after almost seventy years of educating Nashua young people, sometimes as a High School, most recently as a Junior High School, has now been demolished to provide a site for the new courthouse. School buildings, like people, have only a certain life expectancy. A Marchand photo, taken when the school was comparatively new.
NPL file

1967: On February 20 the old Congregational Church at Main and Pearson burned down. It had been used as a Free Will Baptist Church, then became a movie house, the Park Theater, and finally a hardware store. The telephone system inaugurated direct dialing and everyone had to get used to putting "88" before the number.

1968: Throughout the sixties intense controversy boiled over the question of the need for a new library building. The Hunt Building for several years had been inadequate for an expanding collection and modern services. In this year Eliot Carter and his wife, Edith, caused a sensation when they appeared before an Aldermanic meeting and announced the gift of $800,000 toward a new library. The following year the Carters augmented this with an additional $300,000. In April a silent march was held in tribute to slain Martin Luther King.

1969: "Tears and cheers" greeted returning Nashua Battery B, National Guard, from combat service in Vietnam. In the November election, a woman, Alice Dube, was elected to the Board of Aldermen. In February of this year over fifty-five inches of snow fell. In May the Nashua Mall, built on former farmland, was opened.

1970: Census returns showed a population of over 55,000 for Nashua, with large increases for surrounding towns. The Board of Aldermen authorized the creation of Mine Falls Park system. In September schools were closed for almost a month because of a teachers' strike. The new bridge was finally opened to traffic and was named the Veterans Memorial Bridge. New library now a certainty. Anheuser Busch brewery in Merrimack began operating.

1971: Mayor's term of office now four years. Voting machines introduced. In August President Nixon visited Nashua. In September a large crowd attended dedication ceremony for new Nashua Public Library on Court Street. Vocational-Technical College completed on Amherst Street.

1972: One-way street system introduced. In the ongoing school construction program, Birch Hill and Main Dunstable Elementary schools were finished. The Nashua Historical Society held a dedication and open house for its beautiful new Speare Building on Abbott Street.

The Centennial Parade, on a very hot day in late June 1953, was a happening that few who saw it will ever forget. The Ferko String Band came from Philadelphia and showed cheering Nashuans how the "Mummers" march in that city. A year later the Ferko group returned to help in fundraising for the Centennial Swimming Pool.
Courtesy of Frank Mooney

1973: The Arts and Science Center moved into its new quarters, the renovated Central Fire Station, to which the Carter Gallery had been added on the north side. After much discussion concerning the site, the new High School was started at Mill Pond. The Sagamore Bridge was opened to traffic.

1974: Bad fire at Alvirne High School in Hudson. Wyman-Durkin "closest election in history." Severe gasoline shortage, with long lines of cars at filling stations.

1975: New Nashua Senior High School held an open house on October 26. The High School band made a very successful trip to the Cherry Blossom Festival in Washington, D.C., winning an award.

1976: In July fire completely destroyed St. Louis de Gonzague Church. President Gerald Ford visited the city, addressing the Chamber of Commerce. The Bicentennial Parade on June 13 was a joyous event; a monument of granite in the shape of the state of New Hampshire was unveiled at Bicentennial Park overlooking the river.

1977: Mayor Sullivan resigned because of poor health. In the November election Maurice Arel won an easy victory as mayor. Nashua received a windfall grant from the Economic Development Administration—6.5 million dollars. This would be spent for many improvements and amenities including a district courthouse, public works garage, and police station.

1978: Death of ex-mayor Dennis J. Sullivan. Nashua received 11 million dollars in federal housing funds. Pennichuck allowed to tap Merrimack River as additional source of water. New St. Louis de Gonzague Church dedicated. Nashua Historical Society bought Daniel Abbot's house, the Abbot-Spalding House. The first full-length history of Nashua in eighty years, *The Nashua Experience*, was published by the Nashua Public Library. President Carter visited Nashua in February.

1979: Controversy over Nashua High School library subscribing to *MS* magazine became a nationally discussed censorship case. Maurice Arel won election to full four-year term as mayor.

Sincerely yours,

Lester H. Burnham

Lester H. Burnham
Mayor

Lester H. Burnham, an insurance executive, was mayor of Nashua in the centennial year and presided over the many festivities which included a pageant. NPL file photograph

1980: During the presidential primary campaign the Reagan-Bush debate at the High School gymnasium made headlines—Reagan told the *Telegraph* editor who was the moderator: "I paid for this microphone, Mr. Breen." There was a major strike at Nashua Corporation. Hazardous waste dumps became a matter of great concern, with attention focussed especially on the one discovered on Gilson Road. Planning was begun for mass transportation. Studies were under way for two hydroelectric plants, one at Jackson Dam and one at Mine Falls. The Historic District Commission was formed.

1981: 345 air traffic controllers in Nashua affected by strike. Temple Street and Crowley schools closed. Dr. Norman Crisp School on Arlington Street dedicated, replacing on the same site the old Arlington Street School; solar heating was an innovative feature. The December 29 issue of the *Telegraph* carried a list of property assessments. Arel Manor at Lake and Pine streets was ready for tenants. The Main Street Amenities Program included brick sidewalks.

1982: Canal Street was completely rebuilt; cobblestones from one hundred years before came to light. City Hall interior was renovated. Main Street Bridge was remodelled. A plaque on the sidewalk reads as follows: "These improvements were undertaken to commemorate the joining of the north and south portions of our city at this historic point and to recognize the importance of the Nashua River in our lives, past, present and future." Indian Head Bank started construction of a seven-story office building to be called Indian Head Plaza. The Odd Fellows Building was renovated and renamed the Landmark Building. The former Universalist Church was remodelled into a modern office building to be called City Plaza.

1983: Matthew Thornton Health Plan opened its East Hollis Street branch, making effective use of an old brick structure that was once the Holbrook and Marshall wholesale grocery warehouse. New Senior Center finally opened on Temple Street. Planning begun for a circumferential highway to divert traffic from Nashua's Main Street.

179

In the fall of 1950, when morale concerning the local economy was still low because of the Textron pullout, the Chamber of Commerce put on a week-long industrial exposition to demonstrate the potentials for business growth.
NPL file photograph

1984: The year of four mayors. Maurice Arel resigned to become director of the Pennichuck Water Works. Thomas Kelley and Thomas Leonard both served as interim mayors. James Donchess won a December election and was immediately sworn in as mayor. Nashua woman stabbed to death at Simoneau Plaza. Ex-governor of Massachusetts, Endicott Peabody, moved to area, opening law practice in Nashua. William Quigley appointed chief of police to succeed retiring Craig Sandler.

1985: Plan to build new county Superior Courthouse in Nashua approved. Nashua declared the most expensive housing market in state. The Pirates, Nashua's franchise baseball team, announce they will stay through 1987.

1986: The long-awaited Pheasant Lane Mall opened in South Nashua. Nashua-New Hampshire Foundation closed operations. NFS Savings Bank started renovation and enlargement. Mayor Donchess reelected. Year of decision on new Junior High site. Nashua High School boys' basketball team state champions. Problems of homeless focus of concern.

1987: New England Playworld forced to close. Nashua High School girls' basketball team ranked No. 1 in country by *USA Today*. Asbestos dumps found in more places. Citybus bought new buses. Downtown Development Corporation formed. Mayor Donchess led fight against drug dealers; several raids carried out.

1988: Pennichuck Junior High School dedicated. Kindergartens now part of public school system. Final approval for Hall's Corner project; over a period of ten to twenty years 643 acres will be developed, involving 3,450 housing units. Consortium led by John Stabile set up trust to preserve forest land. Nashua Art Association held thirty-fifth Greeley Park exhibit. Summer marked by

abnormally hot weather. Teachers' strike averted after weeks of negotiation. Chemical leak at W. R. Grace plant raised questions of safety. Drug busts on French Hill and Palm Street area continued. Harbor Homes received grant for housing for the homeless. Trafalgar Square office complex completed. A beautiful and impressive new hotel, the Clarion-Somerset, opened in this location off Amherst Street. An inspiring note was the rehabilitation of the well-known bag lady, Lillian, through efforts of one concerned individual. Judd Gregg elected governor in November election. At the end of the year Nashua looked forward to continued prosperity and growth. The Nashua Trust Company announced plans to build a new headquarters at East Hollis and Main streets. This bank will celebrate its one hundredth anniversary in the spring of 1989.

Conclusion

It is Christmas Eve in the year 1895. The editor of the *Daily Press* looks out his window at a light snow falling on Main Street, then goes back to his desk to write an editorial on friends who have recently died, friends whom he is missing deeply. After sounding his roll call of people who have helped to build the city of Nashua, he concludes with this paragraph:

But what of the future? It is ours to make. We shall not fulfill our destiny unless we emulate the virtues of these men who built better than they knew. Peace to their ashes, and good will and prosperity in Nashua and elsewhere is the wish of the city editor on this Christmas Eve.

The Good Cheer Society was founded in 1885 in response to a need for volunteers to make home visits to persons who were ill or housebound by disabilities. It soon expanded into a visiting nurse service to give home care. Good Cheer caramels are still made and sold every year as a fundraising project. In this photograph, probably taken in the early fifties, are seven members of the Board of Directors. From left to right: Kay Atherton, Helen Smith, Muriel Thurber, Helen Richards, Edith Goodhue, Geraldine Bickford, and Hazel Rollins. Courtesy of Nancy Atherton Buell

*St. Joseph's Orphanage served homeless
children of the area from 1900 until 1963.
The orphanage and its adjoining chapel
were located on Main Street between Otter-*

son and Belmont streets. In these photos Christmas at the orphanage is depicted, complete with a visit from Santa Claus. Courtesy of Alfred Lawrence

A graduation class at St. Stanislaus School, date not known, looks expectedly out at the camera. Father Eugene Dranka stands at right. This church, serving the Polish community of Nashua, was built in 1909 on Franklin Street. The white church gives a touch of European feeling to the downtown area.
Courtesy of Alfred Lawrence

A class of young students at St. Christopher's School poses on the church steps in 1954. Every one of them is showing his or her very best demeanor. They represented, as do all children at any time, the best hope for the future.
Courtesy of Alfred Lawrence, the father of one of the children

*This happy group was taking part in the
annual "West End Reunion" of members
and former members of the Greek churches.
The date of the photo was 1952; the site of
the reunion was the grove where in 1973
Saint Philip Greek Orthodox Church
would be erected and dedicated.
Courtesy of John Lafazanis*

Union Station was razed in 1965, as the days of local railroading seemed to be coming to an end. Built in 1860, it was a landmark that many people were sentimental about. It was connected with so many memories in the lives of individuals: going away to college, starting on a vacation trip, taking shopping trips into Boston, not to mention commuting every day to an out-of-town job.
Courtesy of Frank Mooney

Until sites adjoining the Simoneau Plaza mall were cleared for its construction, this house, built in 1847, stood at the edge of the road. Its history is a throwback to the days of taverns and coaching. Originally the Marsh Tavern was on the same site. Rebuilt as a residence, it was known as the Morrill House. The first owner paid for the house by his earnings in the gold fields of California. Many people were saddened by its demolition but at the time there was no organized preservation group that could have come to its rescue and have it moved.
NPL file photograph

The building that had been on the corner of Park Street and Main since 1872 burned down in 1961. Its chief tenant at the time was the Bargain Outlet where many mothers shopped for school clothes. The Allen Building is now on the site. Courtesy of Alfred Lawrence

There has been a Camera Club in Nashua for a long time. Here is an interesting mix of people who attended an outing given by the club for members and their families and friends, probably in the early 1950s.

Although no identifications have been made for this picture, perhaps some of the individuals will find themselves in it. Courtesy of Alfred Lawrence

On June 27, 1961, this photograph was taken to show progress on a federal housing project in the Burke Street area. When completed the project would be called Vagge Village, in honor of the popular mayor, Mario Vagge. This was only one of several housing developments for low income families that were built at this period.
Courtesy of Alfred Lawrence

The Pilgrim Congregational Church, replacing the old Olive Street Church in 1882, in its turn stood at the top of Temple Street for over seventy years. Hurricane Carol in 1954 caused severe damage to the church and the congregation decided to build a new church. In 1956 Pilgrim Church was moved from the site; some of its materials were incorporated into the new church on Watson Avenue. The Indian Head Bank bought the site and today Indian Head Plaza and its parking lot occupy it. This unusual photograph shows how the rear of the Pilgrim Church was constructed, along with a house formerly on Church Street.
Courtesy of Frank Mooney

Four employees of Greenerd Press pose beside their machines. They are, left to right, Philip Laflamme, Eugene Madden, Mr. Kendall, and John Doherty.
Courtesy of Alfred Lawrence

Employees of Sanders Associates and their families enjoy a performance at Boston Garden in 1960. A few of the people have been identified. They are, front row, left to right: Mr. and Mrs. Ray Chaput and their niece; and at right end Mr. and Mrs. Tom Arnold and their three children. Second row: Mr. and Mrs. Dick Cardin and their two children; and Mr. Ford.
Courtesy of Alfred Lawrence

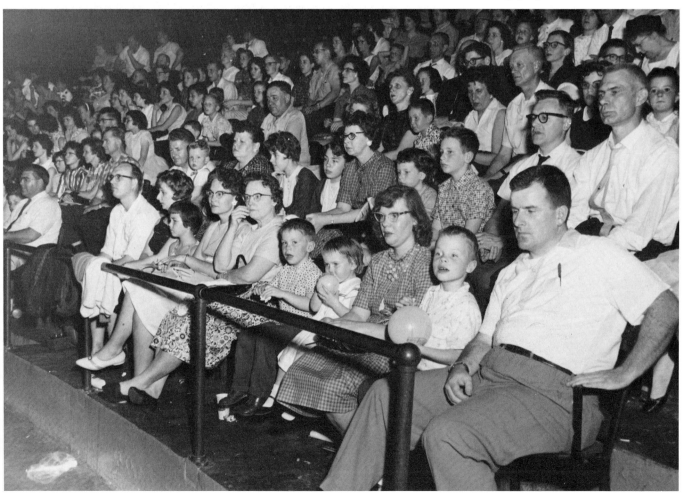

The Walnut Street Oval is seen here just before construction began on the District Courthouse in 1977. In former days the Nashua Manufacturing Company had planted trees around the edge of this circular piece of land as a green spot in the midst of the mill buildings.
Courtesy of Robert Frost

Looking down on Main Street in 1977 revealed heavy traffic conditions that still persist. Traffic is undoubtedly Problem Number One on the list of municipal headaches.
Courtesy of Robert Frost

People are so accustomed to the brick sidewalks that the inconveniences during the time they were being installed are almost forgotten. This snapshot will not arouse nostalgia but it does give an example of the difficulties of a walk downtown during that period of change.
Courtesy of Robert Frost

The Gage Hotel on Olive Street stood directly behind the Court Street Post Office. A modest establishment, known simply as "the Gage," it was operated by a succession of women proprietors from 1905 until 1970 when it was torn down to make way for the new library. In the last few years of its existence an addition on its south side housed the offices of the Degasis Insurance Agency. Many people regretted the loss of a small, homey place where single persons could find respectable lodging near downtown. As a symbol of the character of this little hotel, note the rocking chairs on the porch!
Courtesy of Alfred Lawrence

Pop Warner football has been a feature of the juvenile sports scene since the fifties. Here are the 1972 teams. Bambino baseball in recent years has become another sports activity for youngsters. In 1988 Nashua was host to the World Series for Bambinos.
Courtesy of Alfred Lawrence

191

This sketch by Natalie Roode was drawn
for a brochure about District School
Number 1, prepared by the King's Daughters Benevolent Association which restored
the school in 1976 as a bicentennial
project. The brick school is beside the Old
South Burying Ground near Royal Ridge
Mall. (A photograph of the school appears
in Chapter One.) The original District
Number 1 school was destroyed by fire and
rebuilt in 1841. It was part of the Nashua
school system until 1921. It is now used as
a "Living History" lesson for fourth grade
children who spend a day going to school
under the same conditions as pupils did
during the eighty years when the school
was actually in operation.

The Jackson Dam has played a colorful part
in Nashua's history. The very first dam at
this point was built in 1815; a sawmill was
set up at one end and a gristmill at the
other end. After the Jackson mill was
started a dam was built to provide water
power for it. In 1847 the company built a
replacement; by 1878 this, too, had decayed
and another wooden dam was put in its
place. The present concrete dam was built
in 1907. It was considered a great engineering achievement for its time; newspaper
articles followed its construction closely
and went into detail concerning the
problems involved. It was not equipped,
however, with a fish-way as was the
previous dam; presumably fish had aban-
doned the Nashua River by the early part
of the century and were no longer going
upriver to spawn. In this photo we see a
rare phenomenon—the uncovering of the
skeleton of one of the old wooden dams
when, on May 1, 1983, the river was held
back so that the condition of the dam could
be examined. This was done in connection
with the starting up of the new hydroelectric installation.
Courtesy of Gerry Blanchette of Anderson-
Nichols Company, Concord

Floods, when the Nashua River has threatened to rise above its banks, have occurred periodically. In this older picture curious spectators watch as debris from upriver goes over the falls into the churning maelstrom below.
Courtesy of Alfred Lawrence

The worst flood in Nashua history was the catastrophic one in 1936. Again, in this picture, spectators watch in awe as the broiling waters completely engulf the Jackson Dam. Great damage occurred to homes and industries in this inundation. The 1936 flood almost ranks with the fire of 1930 as a major calamity that hit Nashua.
NPL file photograph

Two photographs taken in the spring of 1987 graphically illustrate the power of the river in flood time. The waters rose to very high levels but by no means matched the big overflow of fifty-one years before. In the first photograph the turbulence at the foot of the dam is shown; the cocktail lounge of the River Club had several feet of water on its floor.
Courtesy of Kathy Seward-McKay, photographer, and the Telegraph

The second photograph looks down on the Sanders plant on Canal Street as the waters seem to encircle it.
Courtesy of Kathy Seward-McKay, photographer, and the Telegraph

194

Rachel Sanborn, 1905-1986. There is no formal portrait of Rachel available, but she herself probably would have preferred this picture showing her at work. It was taken in 1954 in honor of the eight millionth book circulated by the Nashua Public Library. Rachel had worked for forty years at the library when she retired in 1970. She was a dedicated and resourceful reference librarian who especially enjoyed helping students. A person who had read deeply, she had high standards as to what constituted literature.
Photograph by Fotomart; NPL file

Elizabeth C. Spring, 1906-1986, is shown here as she looked in her later years when she was still active. She was a member of the staff of the library for almost forty years. Elizabeth, known to her friends as "Libby," was on the Board of Directors of the Hunt Homes and also worked for the New Hampshire Federation for the Blind. She gave many hours of service to the Nashua Historical Society. Talented in the field of juvenile writing, she was the author of a young people's novelette about Nashua history, "Obadiah Comes Fourteen."
NPL file photograph

Anne M. McWeeney, 1899-1988, was a teacher who, like David Crosby, was an honor to the profession. A native of Nashua, she taught at Nashua High School for forty years and was chairman of the English Department on her retirement. Anne taught swimming for many summers to Nashua children and retained this interest well into her later years. She was a shining example of a person who surmounted many physical problems to continue an active life of community involvement. She was one of the people who helped make Nashua a better place in which to live. Her death in August 1988, shocked many friends because they never thought of her as "old."
Photograph by Bradford Bachrach; courtesy of Alice McWeeney

"Then and Now"

From 1840 to 1881 the middle of the south side of Park Street was the location of the Nashua Literary Institute, David Crosby's private high school where many Nashua citizens received an education. In this photo the students are assembled on the steps.
NPL file photograph

Now the site of the Crosby school is the parking lot for the Slawsby Insurance Company.
Photograph by Brian Lawrence

During the last half of the nineteenth century and until 1922, the corners of West Pearl Street and Main looked like this, with the Parkinson Building on the south corner and the Tremont House on the north. When the photograph was taken around 1875 George Little's grocery store was in the Parkinson Building.
NPL file photograph

Miller's popular store stands on the south corner today as it has since 1968. This store started out around the corner on West Pearl Street. The bank building that was built in 1924 as the Second National Bank is now, of course, the Bank of New Hampshire.
Photograph by Brian Lawrence

At the corner of Eldridge and Main streets, bay-windowed houses stood. The one on the right was the Holman residence. Charles Holman, whose life story was literally "from rags to riches," developed a large confectionary business on Eldridge Street. His son gave the money to build Holman Stadium in memory of his parents.
NPL file photograph

Now St. Patrick's Center occupies the same sites. It was built by St. Patrick's Church in the 1960s.
Photograph by Brian Lawrence

Then, Mt. Pleasant School had a tower. The first school built by the town of Nashville on this site burned down in 1869; this much larger one was built in its place. In 1925 the present school was built after the old one was torn down.
NPL file photograph

Now the 1925 school has been beautifully renovated and enlarged. Pupils went to school in temporary classrooms, including space at the Center for the Arts, during the year that this work was going on. In the fall of 1987 Mt. Pleasant was reopened.
Photograph by Brian Lawrence

The Nashua Public Library was dedicated on September 28, 1971, on a site at the corner of Court and Park streets that had been previously scheduled as an urban renewal project. In providing space for the library and a large courtyard area, many former houses were removed and Olive Street vanished from the map. The new building has proved its worth many times over and should serve several generations yet to come.
Photograph by Bruce Marks

The west wing of the library, on its second level, was provided in the original plans as expansion space for the future. That future has now arrived and the library administration and trustees are planning very soon to develop the area. It is anticipated that the Music/Art/Media Department will be moved to this downstairs space to relieve congestion on the main floor.
Photograph by Bruce Marks

The Nashua Center for the Arts occupies the former Central Fire Station. The renovations made in 1970, when the Center moved in, included the Carter Gallery that was added to the north side. At that time the institution was called the Nashua Arts and Science Center. Under the direction of Steve Jones, its present executive director, the Center has increased the number of its exhibits. It offers a regular schedule of classes in all of the arts. The photo shows a young group of performers in the 1987 season of Kids Into Drama.
Courtesy of Steve Jones

The Nashua Symphony Orchestra is now in its sixty-fifth year. It has been widely praised as a brilliant musical organization and its concerts are always sellouts. Along with the Nashua Choral Society, also administered by the Nashua Symphony Association, it brings the joy of live music to the area. The orchestra also performs at community events such as the annual Fourth of July festivities in Holman Stadium. Somehow, the fireworks always seem more exciting when introduced by the orchestra's rendition of the 1812 Overture! The orchestra gives music appreciation programs in the public schools. The present conductor is Royston Nash. Kent Werth is the new conductor of the Choral Society.
Courtesy of Kathy Asta

201

The Soldiers and Sailors Monument has stood on Abbott Square for one hundred years. It was dedicated on October 15, 1889, in an impressive ceremony attended by Civil War veterans from all over New England. The cornerstone had been laid on the previous Memorial Day by the Grand Lodge of Masons of New Hampshire. The monument was designed by T. M. Perry, an architect for the Quincy, Massachusetts firm that erected it. Its foundation is eleven feet deep. The total height of the monument is fifty-two feet. The only damage it has suffered in its century of existence is the loss of the sailor's sword.
NPL file photograph

SOURCES OF INFORMATION ON • NASHUA HISTORY

There have been three full-length histories of Nashua published during the last 150 years. They are:

Fox, Charles J. *History of the Old Township of Dunstable.*
Gill, 1846; Heritage reprint, 1983 (has index).
Parker, Edward E., Editor. *History of the City of Nashua, New Hampshire.* Telegraph Publishing Co., 1897.
Nashua History Committee. *The Nashua Experience: History in the Making, 1673-1978.* Phoenix Publishing, 1978. Copyright Nashua Public Library.

There have been several commemorative booklets published, of which two are noteworthy for the amount of historical information they offer. These are:

Official Report of the Semi-Centennial Celebration of the City of Nashua, New Hampshire. Telegraph Publishing Co., 1903. Well illustrated.
Nashua Centennial: The Story of a Century, 1853-1953.
Cole, 1953. Useful chronology in spite of a few factual and typographical errors.

For genealogical information, the following publications are useful:

Hill, John B. *Bicentennial of Old Dunstable.* Spalding, 1878.
Stearns, Ezra S. *Early Generations of the Founders of Old Dunstable: Thirty Families.* Little, 1911; Heritage reprint, 1986.
Works Projects Administration. *Genealogies* (2 volumes).
Unpublished manuscript at Nashua Public Library.
Nashua City Reports. From 1887 until 1935 the city reports included vital statistics listings of births, marriages, and deaths which are often helpful in tracing an individual.

For information on the Nashua Manufacturing Company and the Jackson Mills, the following sources are suggested:

Archives of the Baker Library, Harvard Business School, Boston, Mass. Primary documents on the cotton mills were deposited here when they closed. It is advisable for researchers to arrange ahead of time with the library if they wish to peruse these voluminous materials.
MacGill, Caroline E. *The History of the Nashua Manufacturing Company.* Unpublished manuscript is on file at the Nashua Historical Society. Published in the *Nashua Telegraph* in June 1923.
Work Projects Administration. *List of Active Industries.*
Unpublished manuscript circa 1938 at Nashua Public Library.

For information on the Nashua-New Hampshire Foundation, Stephen Winship is the author of a history of the organization which will be published in 1989.

For information on the French-Canadians in Nashua, an excellent source is the following:

Theriault, George F. *Franco-Americans in a New England Community: An Experiment in Survival.* Harvard University, Ph.D. thesis, 1951. Now available in published form.

For access to material in the *Nashua Telegraph*, the following are suggested:

Nashua Telegraph 150 Anniversary. Published by the newspaper in 1982.
Chronological notes compiled by Elizabeth C. Spring for the above publication are available at the Nashua Public Library and are often helpful in tracing information on a specific subject.
The Reference Department of the library maintains an index, starting in 1971, to local events in the *Telegraph*.

A comprehensive bibliography can be found on pages 262 and 263 of *The Nashua Experience.*

●

INDEX

ABOUT THE AUTHOR

Florence Crosby Shepard has lived in Nashua for the past forty years. She is a graduate of the University of New Hampshire and obtained a degree in Library Science from Simmons in 1971. After twenty-eight years service at the Nashua Public Library, she recently retired. Her previous work in local history was as editor of *The Nashua Experience,* published in 1978. In 1988 she was named the first recipient of the Mayor's Award for Superior Achievement in Arts and Letters. She is a descendant of Simon Crosby who emigrated from Yorkshire, England, in 1635. Ms. Shepard has four children and seven grandchildren.

•

ABOUT THE PHOTOGRAPHIC EDITOR

Brian Lawrence is employed at *Cameraland,* a photographic store on Nashua's Main Street that has been owned and operated by his family for many years. He is a graduate of Nashua High School, class of 1978. His skill at copying old photographs was learned from his father. Much of his work is in commercial photography. Brian is the father of two children. This snapshot of him was taken by the author while he was photographing some of the gravestones at the Old South Burying Ground.

•